# HIDDEN HISTORY

*of* CIVIL WAR

# WILLIAMSBURG

# Hidden History

## *of* CIVIL WAR

## WILLIAMSBURG

### Carson O. Hudson Jr.

THE
History
PRESS

Published by The History Press
Charleston, SC
www.historypress.net

*Front cover (clockwise from top left)*: Major General George B. McClellan. *Library of Congress*; Confederate general Joseph E. Johnston. *National Archives*; Lieutenant George A. Custer, May 1862. *Library of Congress*; A watercolor of Union wagons and troops passing through Williamsburg on May 9, 1862. *Library of Congress*.

*Back cover*: Company C, Sixth Maine Infantry. These men fought at Williamsburg in May 1862 and later marched through the town on the road to Richmond. *Library of Congress*.

First published 2019

ISBN 9781540239358

Library of Congress Control Number: 2019935350

*Notice*: The information in this book is true and complete to the best of our knowledge. It is offered without guarantee on the part of the author or The History Press. The author and The History Press disclaim all liability in connection with the use of this book.

*For two forgotten ancestors who were present during the fighting at Williamsburg, Virginia, on April 11, 1863:*

*Grief Carr Hudson*
*Company K, Twenty-Sixth Virginia Infantry*
*Died May 22, 1864, of wounds received at Bermuda Hundred*

*William Harrison Hudson*
*Company K, Twenty-Sixth Virginia Infantry*
*Captured at Hatcher's Run, March 29, 1865*

# CONTENTS

| | |
|---|---|
| Preface | 9 |
| Acknowledgements | 11 |
| | |
| Prologue | 13 |
| Secession | 16 |
| The First Confederate Military Hospital | 22 |
| A Williamsburg Mardi Gras | 25 |
| A Suspected Spy | 29 |
| The Wedding Gown Flag | 32 |
| The Refugees | 35 |
| Retreat, Battle and Abandonment | 37 |
| The Photographers | 49 |
| Colonel Ward and the Floridians | 52 |
| Kearny the Magnificent | 55 |
| Sarah Edmonds | 61 |
| The Dead and Wounded | 64 |
| The Unknown Horse | 73 |
| The Confederate Generals | 76 |
| Occupation and Polite Resistance | 81 |
| Sallie Galt | 87 |
| "Yankee" Bowden | 92 |
| The Red-Legged Devils | 96 |
| A Yankee Sutler | 101 |

# CONTENTS

Courtship and a Wedding                                        104
Williamsburg and the Little Bighorn                            112
Emancipation                                                   115
A Confederate Raid                                             120
Mrs. Anderson's Wine                                           123
The Oath of Allegiance                                         126
The War Continues                                              132
The Market Line                                                136
"A Unique Entertainment"                                       139
The Lost Library                                               142
Wistar's Raid                                                  145
The Doctor in Blue                                             151
The Picket Post                                                154
Epilogue                                                       157

Appendix A. Residents of Williamsburg, 1860                    161
Appendix B. The Williamsburg Junior Guard                      197
Appendix C. The Armies of the Battle of Williamsburg           201
Appendix D. The Hospitals of Williamsburg                      207
Appendix E. A Note on Maps of Civil War Williamsburg           211
Appendix F. The Emancipation Proclamation                      215
Appendix G. The Medal of Honor at Williamsburg                 219
Bibliography                                                   223
Index                                                          231
About the Author                                               239

# WHY REMEMBER CIVIL WAR WILLIAMSBURG?

Today, the city of Williamsburg, Virginia, exists in the shadow of the renowned museums and reconstructed historic area of Colonial Williamsburg. Each year, visitors come by the tens of thousands to visit the re-created eighteenth-century town where the founding fathers walked. When visitors arrive, they expect to learn about George Washington and Thomas Jefferson.

Consequently, as I speak to people about Williamsburg during the Civil War, most are astonished to discover that there was a major battle here, numerous skirmishes and raids and a prolonged Federal occupation of several years. Indeed, they are often amazed that there are more Williamsburg stories from the 1860s than the 1760s.

The American Revolution was important, to be sure. Nonetheless, the Civil War is what defined the nation that the founding fathers wrought. The Williamsburg of the 1860s was a time of patriotism and sacrifice, bravery and cowardice, love and hate, slavery and emancipation. In short, what happened in Williamsburg is the story of the United States at a time when we were at war with each other and a microcosm of what was happening across the entire nation.

When I was a graduate student, historians often stated that 620,000 American soldiers died in the Civil War. Using new data, it is now accepted that as many as 750,000 American soldiers—North and South—may have died. That is 500 dead American soldiers, every day, for four years. And that was in a divided country that was one-tenth the present size of the

Main Street of Williamsburg, Virginia, looking east from the College of William & Mary at the time of the Civil War. *Special Collections, John D. Rockefeller Jr. Library, Colonial Williamsburg Foundation.*

United States. Comparatively speaking, if we had the same war today, we would lose 7.5 million soldiers. That is 5,000 dead Americans every day. How would that affect you, your family and friends, your community, your country? This is what Americans—and Williamsburg—experienced more than 150 years ago.

Sadly, a forgotten fact is that the very ground in Williamsburg upon which the founding fathers walked in the eighteenth century was later soaked with the blood of their children and grandchildren eighty years later during the Civil War. Today, visitors walk over it, unaware that it is truly hallowed ground.

History is a collection of stories, anecdotes and bits of trivia about people. This book is an attempt to tell some of the forgotten stories.

# ACKNOWLEDGEMENTS

Historical facts don't change, but often, the interpretation of those facts does. As we dig deeper, new details come to light that affect what we know. I am excited that I can expand upon an earlier work of mine, *Yankees in the Streets*, with this new printing that contains some updates, corrections and many more illustrations. I thank Arcadia Publishing and The History Press for this opportunity. I especially thank Kate Jenkins, acquisitions editor, for believing in my work and for the great assistance she has given me.

As I stated in my earlier work, gathering all the information needed for this volume involved a number of people who must receive thanks from me for their endeavors.

Several friends and associates at the Colonial Williamsburg Foundation were quite helpful with facts and pointed me in the right direction for answers. They include Dennis Cotner, Lou Powers, Pat Gibbs, Linda Rowe, Linda Baumgarten, Gail Greve, Cathy Grosfils, Laura Arnette, Meredith Poole, Emily Williams, Caitlin Burke and Steve Barnes. A special thanks to Marianne Martin, photo archivist with the Colonial Williamsburg Foundation, who graciously gave me her time searching for images.

Anne Marie Millar, former director of education of the Mariners' Museum in Newport News, Virginia, and now manager of outreach education with the Jamestown-Yorktown Foundation, offered advice and opinions.

# Acknowledgements

Margaret Cook and the staff of the Special Collections Department at the Earl Gregg Swem Library of the College of William & Mary were patient with all my requests for documents.

Robert E.L. Krick, of the Richmond National Battlefield Park, graciously shared research material.

Rebecca Rose and Robert Hancock, of the former Museum of the Confederacy (now called the American Civil War Museum) in Richmond, provided information about existing artifacts.

Les Jensen and Tim Smith, both fine historians of the Confederacy and of local Virginia regiments, were generous with their time and encyclopedic knowledge of the Peninsula Campaign.

Particular thanks are given to Drew Gruber, executive director of Civil War Trails, for his involvement in saving and marking the battlefield at Williamsburg.

Finally, I owe a monumental debt of appreciation to Kaylan Stevenson, who made my manuscript readable, and a loving gratitude to my wife, Melissa, who puts up with a husband who spends more time in the past than in the present.

Thank you, one and all.

Carson Hudson Jr.
Williamsburg, Virginia
November 2018

# PROLOGUE

The sun rose bright into a cloudless sky on the morning of May 6, 1862. The last twenty-four hours had been filled with a constant rain, so the warmth of the sun drying everything out was a welcome sight. Mockingbirds appeared and sang out in the woods and fields. Unfortunately, around the old town of Williamsburg, there were many who could no longer enjoy the heat of the sun or the music of a bird. The Battle of Williamsburg had taken place the day before, and there were thousands of dead and wounded soldiers from both the North and the South scattered around the town.

Williamsburg, along with the rest of Virginia, had joined the Southern Confederacy the year before. Now, a Federal army (under General George B. McClellan) was on the Virginia Peninsula attempting to capture the Confederate capital at Richmond and end the rebellion. Unfortunately, Williamsburg stood in the way of the Federal advance. With a battle fought just to the east of town, the inhabitants were getting a close look at what war really meant.

The entire town seemed to be a hospital. Overrun with sick Confederate soldiers in the preceding months, Williamsburg's residents had already converted their churches into hospitals to accommodate those who could not be treated at the two military hospitals located at the Female Academy and the College of William & Mary at either end of the mile-long main street, which was officially called the Duke of Gloucester Street; however, in the nineteenth century, many inhabitants of the town just called it "the main street."

Now, every public building in town became a hospital for the wounded. When that proved inadequate, people opened their private homes, and wounded soldiers were even placed in the open on the public greens. The wounded were everywhere.

With the departure of the Confederate army, Williamsburg also became a town of women, old men and young boys. And with the arrival of Federal troops, the female population of the town had much to say about the current state of affairs. Cynthia B.T. Coleman, residing at the home of her late father, Nathaniel Beverly Tucker, on the town's central green, wrote about the appearance of the invaders as she watched them march up the main street:

> *First in line comes the Artillery as fresh to all appearances and richly comparisoned as though no battle had been fought, no cannon taken the day before. Then follows the infantry in one unbroken line of twenty-eight Regiments with bands of music playing Dixie, Yankee Doodle, Hail Columbia and John Brown's Body. They pass on up the Duke of Gloucester St. which in its time has echoed to the tramp of Hessians, English, French, Continental troops, felt the noiseless foot-fall of the stealthy Indian. The Cavalry possess themselves of the Palace Green covered with its golden shower of buttercups. Supply wagons camp upon the Courthouse Green. Indignant faces look out from behind closed blinds upon the desecration, as they feel it to be, of their beautiful old town.*

Twenty-three-year-old Harriette Cary was even more emphatic in her hatred of the North, writing:

> *The repudiated Stars and Stripes are now waving over our Town, and humiliated I feel, we bow our heads to Yankee despotism. God grant our Southern Patriots may soon relieve us of this degrading yoke.*

Union soldier Alfred Bellard, of the Fifth New Jersey Infantry, wrote of an encounter with one of Williamsburg's female patriots as his regiments passed through the town:

> *We marched through the city, with bands playing and colors flying much to the disgust of the secesh women, one of whom said that she wished we would never get back.*

Most of the Federal troops didn't stay very long. They marched straight through the town in pursuit of the retreating Confederates. Within a month, they would be outside of Richmond and engaged in heavy fighting.

Some Federal troops remained, however, and with the establishment of a Federal provost marshal in town, the city came under martial law. Williamsburg's white females now went out of their ways to irritate their conquerors. Captain Henry Blake of the Eleventh Massachusetts Infantry remembered:

> *The women...took advantage of the uniform courtesy of the 'Yankees',*
> *whom they despised and hated.... They compressed their dresses whenever*
> *they met an officer or enlisted man, so that the garments would not touch*
> *the persons they passed. They pulled their hats over their faces to preclude*
> *scrutiny. But these precautions were useless, for their cadaverous features*
> *and lank forms were sometimes seen; and all were satisfied that the*
> *Southern beauties about whom so much has been written did not reside*
> *in Williamsburg.*

Thus began one of the darkest and most traumatic periods for the old colonial capital. It would last for more than three years. Throughout that time, the town's inhabitants would labor under what they considered to be a "foreign" occupation. Federal troops, in turn, would struggle with the resistant townspeople, Confederate guerrilla raids and the slavery question. The events and daily happenings of this tragic period would affect Williamsburg until well into the twentieth century.

# SECESSION

With the election of Abraham Lincoln in November 1860, seven states of the Deep South, led by South Carolina, decided to leave the Union. By April of the next year, they had formed a government in Montgomery, Alabama, and created a new nation, the Confederate States. Although most Virginians sympathized with their sister states to the south, moderates in the Old Dominion initially kept her from joining the new Confederacy. Several prominent Virginians, among them ex-president John Tyler, attempted to calm the heated atmosphere by calling for a conference to peacefully resolve issues. On April 12, 1861, however, matters took a turn for the worse as Confederate guns opened fire on Fort Sumter in Charleston, South Carolina.

When President Lincoln called upon the states to furnish seventy-five thousand volunteers to put down the rebellion, Virginia's governor, John Letcher, officially informed the president that

> *I have only to say that the militia of Virginia will not be furnished to the powers at Washington for any such use or purpose as they have in view. Your object is to subjugate the Southern States, and a requisition made upon me for such an object -- an object, in my judgment, not within the purview of the Constitution or the act of 1795 -- will not be complied with. You have chosen to inaugurate civil war, and having done so, we will meet it in a spirit as determined as the Administration has exhibited towards the South.*

Virginia governor John Letcher.
*Library of Congress.*

The same day Governor Letcher replied to Lincoln's request, a state convention voted 88 to 55 for a secession ordinance (subject to popular referendum). Southern nationalism had risen to such a point that Virginia was effectively out of the Union.

An inhabitant of Williamsburg, a young widow named Cynthia Beverly Tucker Washington, was in Richmond during the secession convention. She was the daughter of Nathaniel Beverley Tucker, a noted jurist and professor of law at the College of William & Mary, and the granddaughter of St. George Tucker, who had served with George Washington at Yorktown.

Her father, a firm believer in states' rights (and one of the foremost secessionist fire-eaters in the South before his death in 1851), had published a two-volume novel entitled *The Partisan Leader* in 1836. The book had foretold a civil war during which Virginia would be invaded by Federal troops.

Although Nathaniel Tucker had not lived to see the moment, his daughter found herself amidst the great events that would accomplish her father's dream. Cynthia had traveled to Richmond to contract a new edition of her father's work, and upon learning of Virginia's decision to leave the Union, she immediately wrote to her young daughter in Williamsburg:

> *You never saw anything like the number of secession flags, they are flying from the tops of houses and from the windows too.... Tell Mrs. Sully that she must not forget to illuminate my room to-morrow night, for Virginia has gone out, and is a secession state—thank God.*

In Williamsburg itself, the population watched the momentous events sweeping the country with great interest. "Secession" flags began to fly as early as December 1860, when South Carolina left the Union. Students at the College of William & Mary hung banners and flags from several buildings on campus until the college president, Benjamin Ewell, ordered their removal. Born in Washington, D.C., a graduate of the U.S. Military Academy and the brother of future Confederate general Richard Ewell, President Ewell considered himself to be a Virginian but did not favor secession.

*Right*: Cynthia Beverly Tucker as a young woman. In 1861, she married a Williamsburg neighbor, Confederate surgeon Charles Coleman. *Colonial Williamsburg Foundation (used with permission from Mrs. Robert S. Barlow)*.

*Below*: The Wren Building of the College of William & Mary in 1856. This was the college's main building. *Special Collections, John D. Rockefeller Jr. Library, Colonial Williamsburg Foundation*.

However, after the Confederate attack on Fort Sumter, the voters in the state referendum did not echo Ewell's feelings. On May 23, 1861, the citizens of Williamsburg cast their votes 135 to 0 in favor of secession, joining their fellow Virginians in officially carrying their state out of the Union.

As the news spread, Virginia state flags and secession banners now appeared at the town's newspaper office, then throughout the city. But amidst the waving of flags, there was serious work to be done. After refusing Lincoln's call for volunteers, Governor Letcher had issued his own proclamation:

> *I, JOHN LETCHER, Governor of the Commonwealth of Virginia, have thought proper to order all armed volunteer regiments or companies within this State forthwith to hold themselves in readiness for immediate orders, and upon the reception of this proclamation to report to the Adjutant-General of the State their organization and numbers, and prepare themselves for efficient service. Such companies as are not armed and equipped will report that fact, that they may be properly supplied.*

Around Williamsburg, men flocked to the new national flag, the "Stars and Bars," and overnight, the old colonial capital city became a Confederate town. At the college, Benjamin Ewell watched as his students jubilantly decorated the college buildings once again with secession flags and banners. This time, however, he didn't order the removal of the flags. Instead, he quietly offered his military services to the State of Virginia.

Military companies began forming, with many of the town's men of military age joining the Williamsburg Junior Guard, the James City Artillery and the James City Cavalry, among others. Sallie Galt, the sister of Dr. John Minson Galt II, the superintendent of the Eastern State Lunatic Asylum, commented, "I never saw anything equal to the uprising of the people, as one man they defend the 'dear old Dominion.'" For those who were too young to don a uniform, there were other ways to help. Ten-year-old John S. Charles of Williamsburg later wrote of his experiences at this time. As an old man, Charles recalled that the Confederates had taken over a barn at the asylum and constructed "therein additional stables and feed rooms." He remembered:

> *This was used to take care of the horses of soldiers who were absent from duty on account of sickness or other causes. The large number of horses kept there made it necessary to take them to the creek for water. This furnished great sport to many boys of the town (one of them was the writer) who were*

Benjamin Ewell was president of the College of William & Mary in 1861. He opposed secession but became a Confederate colonel when Virginia left the union. *Colonial Williamsburg Foundation.*

*invited to take a horseback ride down to the College Landing, over a mile distant, three times daily for a long period. When this fine sport was broken up by the withdrawal of the Confederates in the spring of 1862, there was great lamentation among the boys of the town.*

On July 4, 1861, the *Richmond Enquirer* made no reference to it being Independence Day but offered this letter from a resident of Williamsburg:

*A word from Williamsburg, I am sure, will be welcome. This antique town—or perhaps I should say, this ancient city—is too intimately associated with the <u>old</u> revolution, too closely identified with Virginia's <u>first</u> struggle for freedom, not to be a place of interest in this, the opening of another era of the "times that try men's souls." In the brave old days of '76, Williamsburg was conspicuous as the theatre of stirring words and exciting scenes. And now, as then, the resolute tramp of men in arms, and the stern, determined mien of patriots enrolled for their "victory or death," impart the true poetic charm of chivalric love of liberty to the old city and its surroundings. The College and the Court House have been converted into* *barracks- illustrative, you observe, of the maintenance by the sword, of the patriotism inculcated, and the laws enforced in times of peace.*

*In this, the most sublime struggle for the principles of liberty the world has ever witnessed, the peninsula between the York River and the James, seems destined to be again the scene of most important acts in the bloody drama of revolution...*

*The old revolutionary redoubts at Yorktown are again <u>in use</u>. Who would have thought it? What dreamer would have dreamed it? The first revolution ended there. God grant the second may close as gloriously on the same sacred spot. We were fighting for liberty then; and we are enlisted in the same cause now. The issue is a mighty one- the prize is priceless- our men are brave- our women are watching with anxious eyes—our cause is just—God is with us, and our success is certain.*

In the heady days of excitement following Virginia's secession, Southern patriotism was as strong in Williamsburg as anywhere in the South, and the citizens of the town had definite opinions about the cause and the "perfidious yankees."

# THE FIRST CONFEDERATE
# MILITARY HOSPITAL

When the war began in 1861, Williamsburg was a quiet little town that time seemed to have passed by. The town, however, was the home of the Eastern State Lunatic Asylum. It had opened in 1773 as the first hospital in the British colonies solely concerned with the care of the mentally ill. In 1861, Williamsburg also became the home of the first Confederate military hospital in the South.

The story began with the secession of Virginia in early 1861, when a former Williamsburg resident, Letitia Tyler Semple, the daughter of former president John Tyler, was in New York City with her husband, James, a paymaster in the U.S. Navy. As he resigned his commission to "go South," they returned to Virginia, where her husband joined the Confederate navy and later served as the paymaster to the ironclad CSS *Virginia*. During their journey homeward, Letitia Semple encountered a friend in Baltimore who pointed out that in the upcoming conflict, more soldiers would die from sickness than from bullets. The suggestion was made that hospitals should be established.

Upon her arrival in Richmond, Letitia Semple seized upon the idea and met with her father, who was about to be elected to the Confederate Congress. Through him, a meeting was arranged with the new Confederate secretary of war, Pope Walker. Explaining her concerns for the welfare of the young soldiers now entering the army, she obtained official permission to establish a military hospital in Williamsburg. For the site, she chose the Williamsburg Female Academy located at the east end of the Duke of

Williamsburg Female Academy, located on the site of the old Virginia capitol building. It was converted into a Confederate hospital in 1861. *Colonial Williamsburg Foundation.*

Gloucester Street. Dating from the late 1840s, the Williamsburg Female Academy sat on the foundations of the old capitol building where, eighty years before, Patrick Henry had spoken out against King George III. With the coming of war, the young ladies of the academy had been sent home, and the building was vacant.

Letitia Semple immediately organized the women of the town to outfit the academy building with seventy-five beds and the appropriate linens. Confederate general Lafayette McLaws, commanding a Georgia brigade near Williamsburg, left an impression of the spirit of Letitia Semple. Upon meeting her for the first time, he stated:

> *I hadn't been in the room more than five minutes, when, if she had said to me, "McLaws, bring me a bucket of water from the spring," I would have done it!*

Confederate surgeons were assigned, and the hospital began receiving its first patients in late May 1861. Sadly, the prophecy given to Letitia Semple concerning sick soldiers proved to be all too correct.

As thousands of Southerners rushed to the defense of their new nation, it was not uncommon for half the men of a regiment to be unfit for duty due to sickness during their first few months of service. These soldiers, fresh to war and military life, were crowded together in makeshift camps under unsanitary conditions, and disease soon made its appearance.

Unfortunately, the seventy-five beds of the Academy hospital would soon prove to be too few. By September 1861, Coppens' Battalion of Louisianans, encamped near Williamsburg, listed fewer than 100 men fit for duty out of 600 men on the rolls. The local Peninsula men of the Thirty-Second Virginia Infantry Regiment fared a bit better but still suffered 47 sick out of 413 men.

Letitia Semple was quickly forced to use the College of William & Mary and all the town's churches to accommodate the number of sick Confederates who came through Williamsburg. In October, a woman of the town noted:

*The Churches are all occupied as hospitals, so our Ministers, Methodist, Baptist, and Episcopalian, have to preach in the Chapel at the Asylum. There are seven hundred and fifty sick soldiers in town so we are kept very busy sending articles of food suitable for the sick to them....You would be surprised to see how strangely Williamsburg looks now, the streets are so crowded. So many hundred being added to the population....We have had since the war commenced, 17 sick soldiers staying with us, and 4 had typhoid fever, and all got well, for which we feel thankful.*

The following spring, the town's hospitals would be overwhelmed with the casualties from the nearby Battle of Williamsburg that occurred on May 5, 1862. On that dreadful day, the entire town would become an emergency medical facility.

As the armies passed on and the focus of the war moved with them, sick and wounded soldiers, both Union and Confederate, were eventually transferred to Fort Monroe and points north. During the Federal occupation, the Williamsburg Female Academy remained a hospital for the Union army and later became a barracks for the provost marshal established in town. By the 1880s, the building was torn down, and the lot remained vacant until the Colonial Williamsburg Foundation began the reconstruction of the original capitol building in the 1930s. Today, visitors to the site will find no plaque or stone telling of the Civil War years, but through the efforts of strong-willed Williamsburg resident Letitia Semple, the suffering of thousands of young soldiers was alleviated.

(For more about the hospitals in Williamsburg, the reader should refer to Appendix D.)

# A WILLIAMSBURG MARDI GRAS

Perhaps some of the most notorious visitors to Williamsburg in 1861 were the soldiers from Louisiana. With the transfer of the Confederate capital from Montgomery, Alabama, to Richmond, Virginia, all indications were that the main theater of war would be in the Old Dominion. Troops gathered from every state of the Deep South, and Louisiana ultimately provided ten regiments and five battalions of infantry for service in Virginia, several of which were dispatched to the Williamsburg area to defend against any Federal invasion.

The arrival of the Louisianans excited quite a lot of interest in the Williamsburg area, and they proved to be a truly exotic group of volunteers. Within their ranks were two dozen different nationalities—from Cajuns and Irish toughs to Polish revolutionaries; there were soldiers of fortune, gamblers, poor farmers and gentlemen planters. Some wore uniforms patterned after the dress of the Algerian Zouaves, with baggy red pantaloons and loose-fitting jackets. Others wore gray militia uniforms or simple homespun butternut. Each of them seemed to have a bowie knife and a devil-may-care attitude toward military discipline. One regiment, for example, hijacked their own train on their way to Virginia and had a drunken spree in Montgomery, Alabama. The city officials had to call out troops with fixed bayonets to contain the intoxicated Louisianans until their officers could arrive and control them.

Even after they established camps in the Williamsburg area, their manners left much to be desired. They killed and ate livestock at a prodigious rate, and one officer stated that after only twelve hours on nearby Jamestown Island, they had managed to "eat up every living thing on the Island but two horses and their own species."

Louisiana soldiers also seemed to have a talent for being arrested and confined. Crimes alleged against them included robbery, desertion, forgery and fighting. In August 1861 alone, the Second Louisiana Regiment reported four fights amongst its men, two of which resulted in stabbings. The military jails around the Williamsburg area seemed to be full of Louisianans.

Along with indulging their wild sides, the troops from the Crescent State liked to have parties. General Lafayette McLaws wrote that they "were giving parties and picnics, singing and serenading." A Williamsburg woman described two such entertainments, noting:

> *The Zouave and Louisiana Regiment gave a brilliant ball at their camp one mile from town, & it being damp with no floor, the next one they gave was at Colonel Munford's (Tazewell Hall). They adorned the house with flags, evergreens &c. & speak of having a series of them during the winter.*

In early 1862, the Louisianans quartered near town offered a "burlesque circus" as entertainment for the people of Williamsburg and introduced Williamsburg to a New Orleans tradition. They collected material for costumes from the ladies around town, and a Mardi Gras parade was staged on the Duke of Gloucester Street with over two hundred "New Orleans boys" who were "rigged out in as fantastic manner as it was possible to accomplish," according to Cynthia B.T. Coleman.

At the City Hotel, also on the main street, several of the revelers carried out an elaborate practical joke on the Confederate commander, General John B. Magruder. In the prewar U.S. army, Magruder, known as "Prince John," had been known to be fond of amateur theatricals. It is still a question, however, if he enjoyed being the target of a theatrical deception. One of the "New Orleans boys" later wrote of the affair:

> *The celebration closed with an entertainment given to Gen. Magruder and his staff at an inn in Williamsburg…Ned Phelps…was a leader in that affair. Another member of the battalion from New Orleans, Billy Campbell…was a splendid make-up of a young girl. Campbell was perfection in this regard, it being almost impossible to detect that he was not a girl. Leaning upon the arm of Ned Phelps, Campbell entered the apartment where Magruder was dining in the Virginia hostelry, and was*

*Above*: Tazewell Hall, the home of John D. Munford, was the scene of several Confederate social events and balls over the winter of 1861–62. *Special Collections, John D. Rockefeller Jr. Library, Colonial Williamsburg Foundation.*

*Left*: Confederate brigadier general John B. Magruder. *Missouri Historical Society.*

*introduced to the General by his friend Ned as Miss Campbell, of New Orleans, on a visit to her brother, a member of the battalion. The scene was most ludicrous to those who were acquainted with the joke. Magruder, with that gallantry which always characterized him, placed "Miss" Campbell on his right hand, who partook liberally of everything that was going, including the liquors. How far this thing would have gone on it is difficult to say, had not some of the boys ripped up a feather bed belonging to the landlord of the hotel and permitted its contents to fall through an aperture immediately above the dining room, calling out at the same time: "This is a Louisiana snowstorm." During the snowstorm Ned and "Miss" Campbell took their departure, leaving the General in doubt as to whether he had been in the company of a live lady or a spook.*

Confusion over "Miss Campbell's" identity aside, the Louisianans made a lasting and memorable impression on the people of Williamsburg.

# A Suspected Spy

A problem facing Confederate authorities in Williamsburg was the possibility of Federal spies or disloyal elements entering the area. In Virginia as a whole, those who held to the old Union were regarded with suspicion, and the authorities in Richmond had imprisoned several persons for political infidelity to the new Confederacy. At least one young man from Williamsburg found himself suspect and was saved only through the intervention of his mother.

In 1860, Virginia Southall was living in Williamsburg with her husband and five of her children, including her son Travis. Around December of that year, Travis left Williamsburg to live in Washington, D.C., and engage in business with an older brother. When Virginia left the Union, young Travis, though he had Southern sympathies, remained in Washington and did not return home until July 1861.

Upon his arrival from "Yankeeland," he was interrogated as to his reasons for being in Washington. The authorities asked why he had remained so long after Virginia's secession and the beginning of hostilities. Not satisfied with his answers, the Confederate provost marshal arrested Travis on suspicion of being a spy. He was immediately taken to Richmond and imprisoned. Fearing for her son, Virginia dispatched a letter to no less than Confederate president Jefferson Davis:

[Williamsburg, Virginia] *August 2, 1861*

*Mr. JEFFERSON DAVIS*

*DEAR SIR: About four weeks ago my son, Mr. Travis Southall, arrived here from Washington where he had been for some months for the purpose of joining a volunteer company. Want of means together with other difficulties attending such a step alone prevented his getting here earlier. So soon as he reached this his home he was arrested, underwent a strict examination, and though the examining officer, Captain Werth, congratulated him on answering every question satisfactorily yet Mr. Southall was the next morning sent off to Richmond without previous notice.*

*From Richmond he has been removed to Raleigh, N.C., and up to the present moment no action has been taken in the matter. What the charges are against him or who makes them we know not.*

*All I ask, Mr. President, is that he may be heard, his case examined into. If he prove guilty, though his mother I can say let him be punished; if innocent let him be discharged at once and join his company. Colonel Ewell gave me permission today to say to you that had Mr. Travis Southall applied to him to join his regiment (and which Mr. Southall certainly would have done had time been allowed him) he would have received him without the slightest hesitation.*

*With this letter, Mr. President, I send some depositions. Please examine them, and if you will remember how guardedly all letters had to be worded to get them through Washington at all you must see that they are of some weight. I could send many more equally strong but feel sure that those will suffice to prove the loyalty of my son. May God bless you, Mr. President, and always lead you to do what is right.*

*Most respectfully,*

*Mrs. V.F.T. Southall*

Included in Virginia Southall's letter were several statements by Travis in which he declared himself for the new Confederacy and proposed to join the local militia company for state service. Rounding out the correspondence were depositions as to the character of Travis Southall signed by leading citizens of Williamsburg and notarized by the mayor, Dr. Robert Garrett.

After considering the petitions, President Davis, through Confederate secretary of war Pope Walker, ordered the immediate release of Travis Southall on on August 10, 1861. Travis gratefully returned to Williamsburg and his mother. To prove his loyalty to the state, he enlisted in Company B of the Third Virginia Cavalry at Yorktown in September 1861. He was promoted to sergeant in 1863 and, as promised, served Virginia until the war's end.

# THE WEDDING GOWN FLAG

Presenting hand-sewn flags to Confederate units amidst speeches and parades became a popular pastime in wartime Williamsburg. In the spring of 1862, for example, ladies of the town gave a flag to Company B of Coppens' Battalion, Louisiana Zouaves, with the word "Remembrance" added in white silk appliqué. Although no oration regarding the presentation of flags in Williamsburg survives, the passion of the time can be observed in these words from a similar ceremony in Louisiana at which ladies presented a banner:

> *Receive then, from your mothers and sisters, from those whose affections greet you, these colors woven by our feeble but reliant hands; and when this bright flag shall float before you on the battlefield, let it not only inspire you with the brave and patriotic ambitions of a soldier aspiring to his own and his country's honor and glory, but also may it be a sign that cherished ones appeal to you to save them from a fanatical and heartless foe.*

In June 1861, Catherine Heth Morrison of Williamsburg presented a beautiful hand-sewn silk flag made from her wedding dress to the Fifteenth Virginia Infantry. The flag, white with a blue border and trimmed with silver metallic fringe, consisted of a circle of ten blue stars on each side with the words "15 REG: VA: Vol." on one side and the single word "HOME" on the other.

Catherine (or "Kitty," as she was called) married Robert J. Morrison, a professor at the College of William & Mary, in 1854. Among her treasured

*Above*: Coppens' Louisiana Zouaves, shown in New Orleans before they arrived on the Virginia Peninsula. *Library of Congress.*

*Left*: Flag of the Fifteenth Virginia Infantry, sewn by Catherine Heth Morrison in Williamsburg using her white silk wedding gown. This is now located in the American Civil War Museum. *Author's collection.*

possessions when she arrived in Williamsburg was her white silk wedding gown, which had been carefully packed away. After taking up residence in nearby James City County, Robert and Kitty Morrison were quite happy. Their son, Thomas, was born in 1855, followed by a daughter, Cate, in 1859.

When Virginia joined the Confederacy, Professor Morrison obtained a commission as a captain in the Quartermaster's Department in June 1861. It was about this time that Kitty Morrison donated her wedding gown and patriotically converted it into a banner for the troops of the Fifteenth Virginia following their participation in the Battle of Big Bethel.

Kitty Morrison's "Wedding Gown" flag, with its reminders of home, was given to the regimental commander, Colonel Thomas August, and was an inspiration to the regiment. A year later, at the Battle of Malvern Hill, Colonel August was severely wounded in the leg. As he was being carried off the field, he made a reference to the white silken flag as he shouted to his men: "Boys, remember you belong to the old Fifteenth Virginia, remember you are fighting for your homes and your firesides. Give them hell, damn 'em!"

The flag survived the war and was regarded with reverence by the survivors of the Fifteenth Virginia. In 1911, the veterans of the regiment held a reunion in Williamsburg. In an address presented by J. Staunton Moore, he remembered the flag:

> *The survivors of the Fifteenth Virginia recall with feelings of pride, that when we arrived in your beautiful and hospitable city fifty years ago, Mrs. Morrison, one of your patriotic ladies on the Campus of old William & Mary presented us with the first flag that ever floated over our heads. It was made from her wedding gowns; I recall its colors were white and blue silk, emblematic of the purity of heart of the giver, and of the heavens above us, whose blessings she invoked on our undertaking. This flag waved on many a battlefield and is endeared to us by many sacred ties and tender memories.... It is our privilege and our pride to assure the ladies of Williamsburg that this flag was never captured.*

Sadly, Kitty Morrison's world would be upended soon after her contribution to the cause. Her husband was soon reassigned as a captain in the infantry and died of camp fever in Williamsburg on October 31, 1861.

Both the Louisiana Zouave flag and Kitty Morrison's "Wedding Gown" flag can still be seen in the collections of the American Civil War Museum in Richmond, Virginia.

# THE REFUGEES

As Federal troops occupied the lower Virginia Peninsula in the summer and fall of 1861, many inhabitants of Hampton and the surrounding counties fled their homes and became refugees. Williamsburg became a temporary haven for these displaced families and was, in fact, overrun by them.

The town's residents were initially unprepared for this influx. With the additional burdens of quartering the army that was slowly gathering in and about Williamsburg and nursing the sick arriving at the town's converted hospitals, the housing shortage became acute. Many of the unfortunate refugees were forced to sleep on the Market Square until quarters or transportation farther inland could be arranged. A resident wrote sympathetically of the refugees' plight:

> *Many families are leaving Williamsburg for fear of the enemy but at the same time many persons are here for protection from Hampton, where not a woman or child remained. Poor creatures they arrived here in the night with not even their clothing & many of them slept on the Courthouse Green but I can assure as soon as morning came & we knew of their distress every door was opened to them.*

In early May 1862, many citizens of the town became refugees themselves as the Confederates abandoned their fortifications at Yorktown and began a general withdrawal through Williamsburg. With the Rebel army retreating

Refugees in Virginia. Families like this fled Federal troops on the lower peninsula and relocated to Williamsburg and beyond. *Library of Congress.*

down the main street of the town, the townspeople were despondent that Williamsburg was to be given up to the enemy, leaving their homes to the invading army. A Union chaplain later described their departure:

> *The scenes described to me by eye-witnesses of the departure of many families from Williamsburg, when they became aware of the retreat of their army from Yorktown, were deeply affecting, and worthy of the pencil of the painter. Families without horses or carriages, impelled by the fear of one or two members of the household, arose and fled to the streets, and were seen in scattered groups all along the highways. The young helping the aged, mothers and fathers bearing little children in their arms, the elder children carrying little bundles of such things as they could bear, and the slaves unwillingly assisting in the flight. Where carriages or wagons could be obtained, they were busily filled with the things that were thought to be most useful, and in the wildest haste they hurried out of the place to a spot of imagined safety.*

Those who chose to abandon homes in Williamsburg would not be allowed to return for more than three years.

# Retreat, Battle and Abandonment

In the spring of 1862, the war came to Williamsburg. In March, General George B. McClellan began the Peninsula Campaign by landing over 120,000 troops at Fort Monroe in Hampton, Virginia. His intent was to advance west, up the tidewater Virginia Peninsula, and capture Richmond before a major Confederate force could be deployed against him. Accordingly, he launched the largest military invasion ever attempted up to that time in the United States. Utilizing over 400 vessels, he transported not only his troops but also 44 batteries of artillery and 14,502 horses and mules, plus the army's supply train, to Fort Monroe.

Advancing cautiously, McClellan was determined to lay siege to the Confederates at Yorktown, the scene of General George Washington's siege and victory over the British in 1781. However, the Confederates, under the command of General Joseph E. Johnston, were not the British. They held their Yorktown lines for almost a month as Union troops toiled to construct siege lines and bring up heavy guns and mortars to begin a massive bombardment of the town. On the evening of May 3, 1862, just as McClellan's onslaught was scheduled to begin, Johnston began withdrawing his army from the defensive lines around Yorktown and set them marching toward Williamsburg.

Johnston had never really wanted to fight at the old colonial tobacco port of Yorktown. Two weeks earlier, in Richmond, he had attended a stormy conference with Confederate president Jefferson Davis. Present at the meeting along with Davis and Johnston were Davis's military secretary, General Robert

*Above*: Major General George B. McClellan. *Library of Congress.*

*Opposite, top*: Map of the major roads between Williamsburg and Yorktown, 1862. *National Archives.*

*Opposite, bottom*: McClellan's headquarters at Yorktown, April 1862. *Library of Congress.*

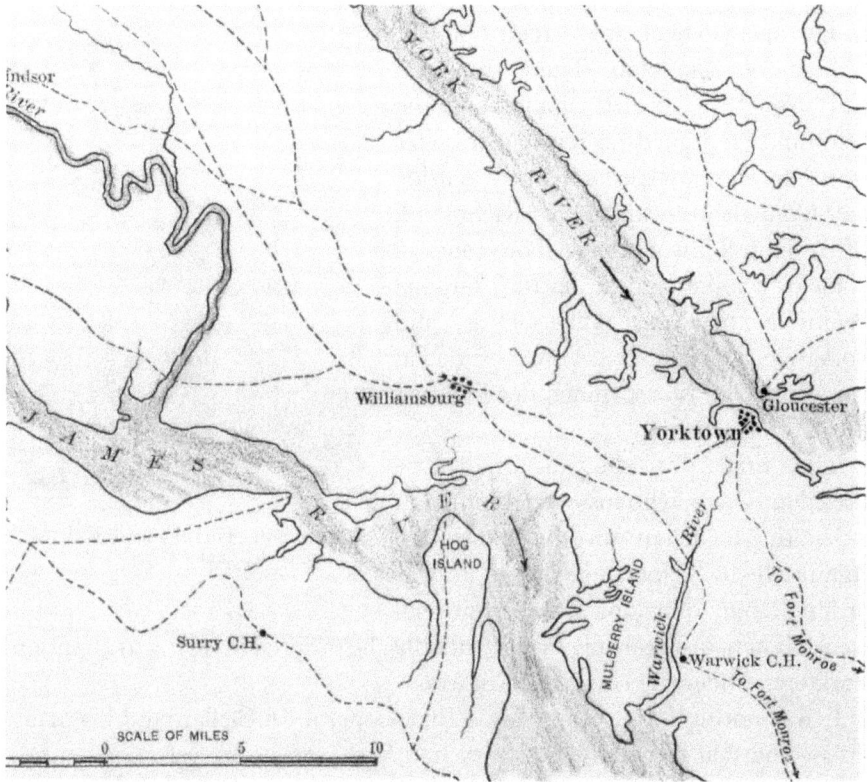

E. Lee and Confederate secretary of war George W. Randolph. There, Johnston had strongly advocated abandoning the peninsula. He argued that it would be better to try to stop McClellan's army outside the Confederate capital of Richmond, where Johnston would have more room to maneuver, rather on the narrow Virginia Peninsula between Williamsburg and Yorktown. The conference finally ended at one o'clock in the morning after fourteen hours of argument.

The final decision was made by President Davis, who instructed Johnston to hold McClellan on the peninsula. Against his will, Johnston did as he was ordered but only for two additional

Confederate general Joseph E. Johnston. *National Archives.*

weeks. Then, disregarding his instructions, he ordered his army to abandon Yorktown under the cover of darkness.

It was not until dawn on May 4 that General McClellan and his army discovered that the earthworks they had faced for weeks were now empty. Around noon, McClellan triumphantly entered the town and proclaimed, "The success is brilliant." Brilliant or not, McClellan had Yorktown, but tactically, he had lost contact with a substantial body of Confederates. He dispatched a cavalry force of two brigades under General George Stoneman up the Yorktown road to Williamsburg to locate the retreating Confederates. After Stoneman's cavalry came four batteries of field artillery and, finally, a supporting force of infantry.

The Yorktown road was in poor shape, however, as it had rained for twenty of the last thirty days. Because of the mud, the lead Confederate units had only made it about twelve miles, just reaching Williamsburg as the Union soldiers at Yorktown discovered they were gone. Although they also had to contend with the mud, the Union troops were a bit faster. Even as they were catching up with the straggling rear elements of Johnston's army, the U.S. Telegraphic Corps were following them, busily planting wooden poles and stringing wire. This road between Williamsburg and Yorktown would eventually come to be known as Telegraph Road.

As the Confederates slipped out of Yorktown, their retreat was covered by cavalry commanded by General J.E.B. Stuart. A Virginian, Stuart had

Union troops beginning their pursuit of the Confederates toward Williamsburg, May 4, 1862. Field drawing by Alfred Waud. *Library of Congress.*

graduated from West Point in 1854 and gone into service with the U.S. Mounted Rifles, fighting Indians in Texas. Later, after transferring to the newly formed First U.S. Cavalry, he served in "Bloody Kansas." In 1859, he had been on leave in Washington, D.C., when word reached President James Buchanan about John Brown's raid on the Federal Arsenal at Harpers Ferry, Virginia. He volunteered as an aide to Colonel Robert E. Lee, who had been ordered to the scene of the insurrection with a detachment of U.S. Marines. There, Stuart had assisted in the apprehension of Brown. As the war began, Stuart had resigned his commission and joined the Confederate army as a colonel of cavalry. Now, a year later, he was a general commanding a brigade of cavalry in Johnston's army.

As the retreat began, Stuart's men kept fires blazing in several locations and maintained noisy activity to mask the Southerners' departure. At dawn, Stuart dispatched some of his men toward the junction of the York and Pamunkey Rivers to watch for Union movement by water from Yorktown. He sent another part of his force, commanded by Colonel William C. Wickham, to protect the army's rear on the direct road to Williamsburg. Finally, he took the last of his brigade and personally covered the old Hampton road to the south. Although the Yorktown and Hampton roads were only a short distance apart, they were separated by dense woods, and both offered a route westward; they converged about a mile outside of Williamsburg.

Confederate major general James Ewell Brown ("J.E.B.") Stuart. *National Archives.*

Throughout the day on May 4, Union cavalry seemed to be in close pursuit of Colonel Wickham's command. There were several small skirmishes on the Yorktown road, and as evening approached, a larger fight developed just to the east of Williamsburg near the major Confederate earthwork of the Williamsburg line, which was known as Fort Magruder.

The pursuing Federal army was getting its first look at Williamsburg and the Confederate defensive works defending the town. A foreign military observer with them noted:

> *The small space of ground on which Williamsburg is built was designed by nature to have an important bearing on the retreat of the Confederates. It was a narrow gate, easily kept closed, through which the whole army had to file in a single column, and which it was necessary to guard against the seizure of the enemy until the last man had passed.*

Colonel Wickham received a serious saber wound in the fighting at Fort Magruder, and command fell to Major William Payne. After a sharp contest, the Confederates around the fort managed to fend off the Union cavalry, and both sides backed off as darkness began to fall.

Meanwhile, General Stuart found that not only was he out of touch with his men on the Yorktown road, but Union cavalry, accompanied by artillery, were actually between him and the junction of the two roads into Williamsburg. Suddenly, he was cut off and had no direct knowledge of the surrounding area. Although he had no reliable map or local guide, Stuart was aware that the James River was directly to the south. After a short skirmish, he turned his men toward the river, as they were less than a mile away. They made it to the James and turned right along the beach. A bit farther to the west, they found the road to Williamsburg from the Kingsmill Wharf. Finally, Stuart's men made their way up Quarterpath Road to the south of Williamsburg. He soon reunited his command around Fort Magruder as the darkness became complete and a heavy rain began.

As the cavalry skirmished around Fort Magruder, the citizens were alarmed over the apparent evacuation of their city without a fight. By this time, most of the Confederate army had managed to pass through the town in its retreat toward Richmond. An Alabama Confederate recorded that "the buildings were crowded with men women & children all of whom wore a countenance of Sadness & deep regret." The appearance of some Confederates must have been equally disheartening. One southern unit, Lieutenant Colonel Paul DeGourney's Independent Battalion of Heavy Artillery, was armed only with eight-foot-long steel-pointed pikes. About 4:00 p.m., they marched down the main street of Williamsburg with their pikes at "right carry arms." One soldier remembered the Confederate commander, General Joseph Johnston, reviewing the battalion as it passed

Confederate major general James Longstreet. Field drawing by Alfred Waud. *Library of Congress.*

"with an approving smile, wondering no doubt, if we had not leaped full armed from the shades of the Middle Ages."

Later that evening, Johnston was outside the town surveying the situation. He determined that he needed to buy more time for his army to make its way down the muddy roads toward the Confederate capital at Richmond. He therefore made a fateful decision for the people of Williamsburg. Johnston ordered the part of his army under General James Longstreet to turn about and delay the Federal advance east of the town until the remainder of the army could get away.

A South Carolina regiment was part of the force ordered to countermarch back through Williamsburg to take up defensive positions outside the city. One Carolinian remembered: "As we passed through the town the citizens were greatly excited, the piazzas and balconies being filled with ladies and old men who urged the men on with all the power and eloquence at their command."

At least one unidentified young lady of Williamsburg attempted to join the fight to defend her town. As a regiment of Mississippi soldiers marched through the streets, she began to harangue them and begged them to turn around and follow her. Just at that moment, the regiment received the order to turn about and double-quick to the sound of the fighting. The young amazon started to the front of the column to take charge when one of the soldiers warned her to stay back or she might tear her dress.

As the rain became heavier, soldiers of both sides fought the mud and tried to stay dry. One Confederate wrote, "It was a very dark night, cloudy and drizzling rain. We nearly ran into the enemy's lines before we knew

The Battle of Williamsburg as seen in *Frank Leslie's Illustrated Newspaper*, May 1862. Engraving from a field drawing by Alfred Waud. *National Archives.*

it." Men in Confederate gray and Union blue took up positions and waited through a miserable night, wondering what the morning would bring.

The next day, May 5, 1862, Federal and Confederate troops became embroiled in a confused and vicious fight just east of town. Although it was later characterized as a rearguard action, the fight at Williamsburg would prove to be the largest battle in the eastern theater since the Battle of Manassas the previous summer.

The town's inhabitants found that the day was just as confusing for them. Chaos reigned in the city. One woman later recalled:

> *All day long we heard the booming of cannon and the rattle of musketry, and yet we hardly seemed to realize at the time how fiercely the battle was raging....All day long the wounded were coming in, they were ministered to by loving hands for all Southern soldiers were our brothers.*

While troops rushed up and down the streets and wounded soldiers were being transported back into town, townspeople climbed to the cupola of the Eastern State Lunatic Asylum to watch the smoke rising from the battlefield. Heartier souls grabbed their umbrellas and ventured onto the fringe of the battlefield.

Seventy years later, a young Hampton refugee, Victoria King, recounted her activities that day giving aid to the Confederates retreating through town, including an encounter with the Confederate commander, General Johnston:

> *I helped to bake biscuits and fry meat for the Confederate army which was retreating before McClellan. On the day that the Battle of Williamsburg was fought, I stood before this house all day passing out biscuits and meat to our men. Joseph E. Johnston, then in command of the Confederate army, passed as we were handing out food. He reined in his horse, waved in our direction, and shouted to the passing troops, "That's what we're fighting for boys."*

Victoria also remembered meeting another Confederate officer that day:

> *As the last of the army was going by, an officer stopped his horse before me, and, handing me his sword, requested that I clean it and save it until he returned. I cleaned the sword—it was a very beautiful weapon—but its owner never came back to claim it. This sword stood in its scabbard…in a corner of the hall for a long time. It was thrown away toward the end of the war by my Aunt Harriet, who was afraid the Yankees would find it, and charge her with aiding and abetting the Confederate cause.*

As the day ended, so did the fighting outside of town. The Confederates had momentarily halted the Federal advance and now continued their

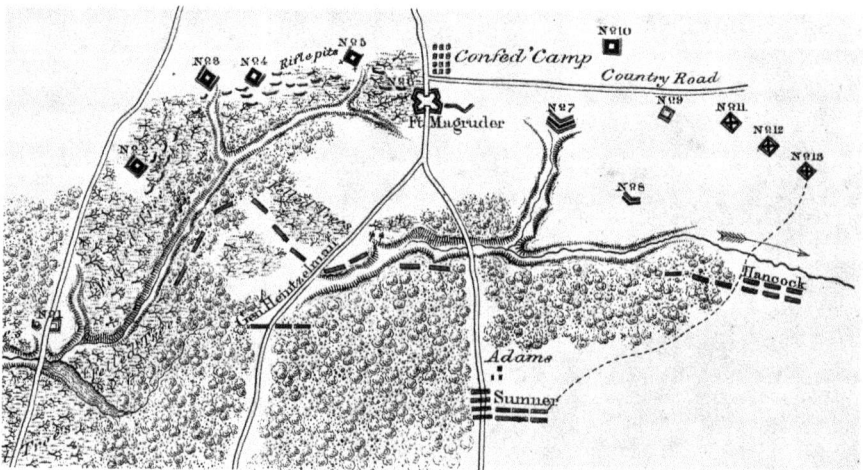

Map of the battlefield at Williamsburg from a postwar U.S. government survey. *National Archives.*

The St. George Tucker House in Williamsburg. This was the home of Cynthia Beverly Tucker Coleman during the Battle of Williamsburg. *Library of Congress.*

retreat through the town. The muddy streets of Williamsburg were filled with wet and exhausted soldiers, mired artillery pieces and frightened townspeople. Stragglers were everywhere, as weary guards shepherded Federal prisoners.

Civilian volunteers, manning a variety of conveyances, attempted to make their way back and forth between the battlefield and the town's hospitals. With the darkness came even more wounded, along with the realization that the Confederates were about to abandon Williamsburg to the enemy. The Tucker House on Market Square was full of tired, wet soldiers. Four brothers of the Eighth Virginia Infantry Regiment shared accommodations in the study, with one falling asleep, exhausted, under the piano.

As the dawn of the next day approached, the rain stopped, and many of the townspeople were faced with a difficult choice—to leave or to stay. Cynthia B. Tucker, who by then was the wife of a Confederate surgeon, Charles Coleman, wrote of the departure of her husband:

> *My sister, a Bride of a few months, had gone off the day before with her husband who was a member of McLaws' division. My husband's Mother and sister had also fled the day before the Battle. He remained with me until the last moment leaving with the rear guard of the Army about sunrise. My Mother, brave woman that she was, decided to remain and take care*

*of her children's home and the wounded who had fallen to her share after the Battle. I determined to stay with her, though my Husband was very reluctant that I should do so.*

The morning of May 6, 1862, promised a sunny day, but Cynthia and other residents of the town were not encouraged. As Cynthia watched her husband and the last Confederates leave, she no doubt captured the sentiment of many of the women who stayed: "We, the women they left behind them, bade them adieu with grave hearts, they to do and suffer, we passively to endure."

Many felt abandoned and could not understand why the whole Southern army had not stayed and fought. Little did they know that the arrival of Federal troops in the city would mark the beginning of what would be more than three years of occupation.

Interestingly, both sides declared victory at Williamsburg. The Richmond newspapers spoke of a great triumph, and Johnston commended General Longstreet for his handling of the battle. The cavalry commander, J.E.B. Stuart, wrote his wife:

*Blessed be God that giveth us the victory, The battle of Wmsburg was fought and won on the 5th. A glorious affair, brilliantly achieved by the rear portion of our army....We were without rations & therefore had to withdraw from the field, leaving our wounded with the ladies at Wmsbg— the enemy was driven from the field entirely.*

McClellan claimed—and the Northern newspapers reported—a win. Although they hadn't broken the Confederate defenses, the Union army had not, as Stuart had written, "been driven from the field." The battle had gone back and forth in the rain throughout the day, but both sides ended the battle close to where they had begun that morning. As the Confederates slipped away to rejoin the rest of their army withdrawing toward Richmond, they left McClellan holding the battlefield. The next day, he would enter Williamsburg unopposed.

# THE PHOTOGRAPHERS

During the fighting that occurred outside of Williamsburg on May 5, 1862, four young photographers sat mired in the mud amidst several wagons on the side of the road leading into town. As they attempted to keep dry in the pouring rain, they watched with great interest as Union troops marched past them toward the sound of the fighting. Occasionally, a Confederate shell would tear through the underbrush and explode, terrifying the horses. Frustrated by the rain and mud, these men, who were working for Mathew Brady, could only sit and wait for the battle to end before they might advance forward and bring out their cameras.

Probably the most well-known photographer of the nineteenth century, Mathew Brady first opened a photographic gallery in New York City in 1844. He quickly prospered as Americans became eager to have their images recorded with the new daguerreotype process. In his early years, he photographed such famous Americans as Daniel Webster, Henry Clay and Edgar Allan Poe. Brady also made the first photograph of a president in office, James K. Polk, and recorded the likeness of past presidents John Quincy Adams and Andrew Jackson for posterity. In 1849, he opened a second gallery in Washington, D.C., which only added to his fame, as everyone who was anyone wanted his or her picture taken in Brady's studio.

By 1861, Brady no longer took many photographs himself. Because of bad eyesight, he now more frequently acted as the manager of his studios and director of operations. With the beginning of the Civil War, he saw an opportunity to preserve history—and, hopefully, to make a profit. At once, he received permission from the War Department in Washington to record the conflict in the field and set about hiring more photographers. Outfitted with wagons, cameras and photographic chemicals, Brady's camera operators would eventually be dispersed to thirty-five different areas of operation.

As General George B. McClellan began his Peninsula Campaign against Richmond in early 1862, a team of Brady's photographers, including James Gibson and John Wood, boarded military transports bound for Hampton, Virginia. Because they had been recognized by Federal authorities as "official photographers," arrangements had been made for the transport of the traveling darkrooms along with their horses and associated equipment.

Upon arriving at Fort Monroe, Brady's men set about their business, photographing everything that attracted their attention—from General McClellan and his staff to the black laborers and teamsters employed by the army. By April, they had departed with the advancing troops and were situated around Yorktown, taking pictures of troops and gun batteries.

After spending almost a month preparing to attack Yorktown, the Federal army awoke on May 4 to discover that the Confederates had abandoned their positions and retreated westward. Gibson and the rest of Brady's team harnessed their horses and joined the line of troops marching up the muddy road toward Williamsburg in pursuit of the retreating Confederates. As evening fell, the party of photographers pulled off the road somewhere between Yorktown and Williamsburg. They ate what little food they had and

A group of Mathew Brady's photographers in the field. *Library of Congress.*

settled down to spend the night in their wagons as it began to rain. All around them, Federal troops lay down and attempted to sleep on their arms as the rain got heavier. With no fires permitted, it was a miserable night for all.

Early in the morning on May 5, the photographers found themselves on the edge of a growing battle. As gunfire exploded in the distance, various Federal regiments and batteries passed down the road beside them. Unable to continue in the confusion, the photographers stayed where they were, listening to the sounds of battle. Eventually, the gunfire died out, and that evening, as wounded soldiers filtered back down the road, the Confederates evacuated their positions and retreated through Williamsburg.

The next day, as the sun came out to dry everything and the Federal army marched into Williamsburg, the photographers inspected the battlefield. Around the major Confederate earthwork known as Fort Magruder, they encountered bodies lying along the road that had been deposited in lines by stretcher-bearers awaiting burial details. One dead Confederate seemed to be aiming his rifle at them, with his weapon resting on a tree stump. Upon inspection, it was found that the man had been shot through the head, apparently while in the act of aiming, and had died with his rifle still in his grasp. After making several exposures, the small party loaded their equipment and entered Williamsburg. That evening, they camped with the troops on the edge of town and enjoyed a warm fire of "Virginia fence rails."

It is not known exactly how long the photographers paused in Williamsburg. Maybe they looked around at the old colonial capital of Virginia and took a few photographs of buildings such as the Bruton Parish Church, the College of William & Mary or the Eastern State Lunatic Asylum. Perhaps they made an exposure of the old Powder Magazine that was, even then, a historic tourist attraction. Possibly they captured an image of the large numbers of Confederate wounded lying around the town or the victorious Union regiments as they were passing down the main street. We will never know. Within a few days, more of Brady's operators arrived on the Peninsula, and the enlarged group divided into two crews to provide greater coverage of the campaign. Several weeks later, they were photographing the Federal army around Fair Oaks just outside of Richmond.

Regrettably, no photographs taken in or around Williamsburg by Brady's men have ever come to light. A search of the Library of Congress, the National Archives and various other public and private collections have not turned up a single image of the town in 1862. One can only wonder what subjects might have attracted the photographers' attention, were photographed and have been lost to history.

# COLONEL WARD AND THE FLORIDIANS

O n the afternoon of May 5, 1862, the Second Florida Volunteer Infantry stood waiting to go into battle outside of Williamsburg. Formed in February 1861 after Florida's secession, the regiment was composed of men from all parts of the state. They had come to Richmond by rail in late July and entered the Confederate capital amidst great celebration on the very day that news of the Southern victory at Manassas had arrived. For the next two months, they guarded Federal prisoners from that battle.

The commander of the Second Florida Infantry Regiment was Colonel George Taliaferro Ward. Born in Fayette County, Kentucky, in 1810, Colonel Ward had settled in Florida before the war and become a prominent voice in the state's politics. As a delegate to the state's secession convention in Tallahassee, he originally opposed secession but went with his state when it became a reality. He stated at that time: "When I die, I want it inscribed upon my tombstone that I was the last man to give up the ship."

Despite Ward's misgivings, the convention's other delegates chose him to be one of Florida's representatives at the Provisional Congress of the Confederate States in Montgomery, Alabama. While serving there, he was commissioned as the colonel of the Second Florida. He immediately joined his new command and proudly took them to Virginia.

Now, Colonel Ward waited on horseback listening to the noise of musketry and cannon as gun smoke rose over the trees. The Floridians were being held in reserve along with the Second Mississippi Battalion. Around four o'clock, however, the Floridians were ordered forward to relieve another regiment on the field. They advanced through town, marching down Williamsburg's main street, led by their colonel. As they passed a house, a young girl called to them to "avenge this blood" as she waved a bloodstained cloth that had come from a wounded soldier. With a yell from Colonel Ward, his men went forward at a run.

The Floridians entered the field and began to form into a line of battle. They were in the process of replacing an Alabama regiment when a misunderstood order caused some men to immediately begin to fall back. In the confusion, both the Alabamians and the Floridians suddenly began to withdraw. The Second Florida quickly broke in "perfect disorder" without ever really forming and began to stream toward the rear. Described as a "brave and gallant man," Colonel Ward attempted to rally his men. While riding into the mass of fleeing soldiers, he was shot dead from his horse. A Florida soldier later wrote of his colonel's death:

Colonel George Taliaferro Ward. From *Memoir of Capt. C. Seton Fleming, of the Second Florida Infantry, C.S.A.* (published in 1884), by Francis Fleming. *Author's collection.*

> *Our gallant and brave colonel ordered a charge and we followed him, but not long was he allowed to lead us (and we would have followed him through thick and thin) for at an evil hour (and when we needed him most) a ball struck him under the left shoulder and come out on the right breast—killing him instantly, he never spoke.*

Ward's death added to the panic of his shaken troops. They ran back almost a mile until they reached a ravine, where they finally formed their ranks. Colonel Ward's body was recovered later that evening by several of his men and carried into town on a blanket. They unsuccessfully tried to find a proper place to leave his remains until around midnight, when they arrived outside the city's courthouse on Market Square. The courthouse had served as an emergency hospital during the day, but now, as the Confederates were leaving the town, the wounded had been evacuated, and the building had literally become a morgue. Colonel Ward's men laid his body on the court clerk's table and pinned a note to his uniform giving his name and rank and asking for a proper burial.

Although the next day was full of confusion amidst the Confederate withdrawal and Federal occupation, Colonel Ward's body was not forgotten. Several women of the town, assisted by Reverend Thomas Ambler of Bruton Parish Church, took the body to the rectory and then to the churchyard. Because no coffin could be had, Colonel Ward was laid to rest wrapped in the blanket that had carried him from the field.

Of his death, Confederate president Jefferson Davis said:

> *Among the gallant and much regretted lost by us was Colonel Ward of Florida, whose conduct at Yorktown had been previously noticed, and of whom General Early in his report of the Battle of Williamsburg says: "On the list of the killed in the Second Florida Regiment is found the name of Colonel George T. Ward, as true a gentleman and as gallant a soldier as has drawn a sword in this war, and whose conduct under fire it was my fortune to witness on another occasion. His loss to his regiment, to his state, and to the Confederacy cannot be easily compensated."*

A month after Colonel Ward's death at Williamsburg, his children received a battle flag of the Second Florida Infantry presented by Florida governor John Milton. Ward's body, however, remained in the Bruton Parish Churchyard. In later years, Cynthia Coleman and other ladies of the town expressed surprise that no one ever claimed his body from its Williamsburg resting place. Thirty-one years after the battle, on May 5, 1893, a monument, donated by citizens of the town, was erected over his grave. Today, Colonel George T. Ward still reposes, as Cynthia B.T. Coleman noted, "neath the soil, in defense of which his life-blood was shed."

# KEARNY THE MAGNIFICENT

P hilip Kearny Jr. led his men from the front. With only one arm, he rode into battle in the manner of the French Chasseurs d'Afrique, waving his sword with his right hand and holding the reins of his horse in his teeth. At the Battle of Williamsburg in 1862, he was certainly one of the bravest and most controversial soldiers on the field.

Kearny was born into a well-to-do New York family in 1815 and was raised by his grandfather. He graduated from Columbia University in 1833 with a degree in law. After the death of his grandfather, he inherited well over $1 million—a huge sum, upon which he could have lived lavishly for the rest of his life. Young Kearny, however, decided that instead he wanted to be a soldier.

He managed to obtain a commission as a lieutenant in the Second U.S. Dragoons and began to learn his new trade under his uncle, Colonel Stephen W. Kearny. Showing promise as a cavalry officer, Philip was sent by the army to observe and study mounted tactics at the prestigious French cavalry school in Saumer. He also took the opportunity to accompany the French expeditionary forces and the Chasseurs d'Afrique into Algiers. There, he distinguished himself in fighting against the Algerian tribesmen to such an extent that the French dubbed him "*Kearny le Magnifique*" (Kearny the Magnificent). Upon returning to the States in the early 1840s, he served as a staff officer to the commander of the U.S. army, General Winfield Scott. Using his experiences in Europe and Africa, he wrote a new cavalry manual for the army.

Brigadier General Philip Kearny.
*Library of Congress.*

When the Mexican-American War began, Kearny raised a troop of cavalry at his own expense. He was promoted to captain and accompanied General Scott's march on Mexico City in 1847. At the Battle of Churubusco just outside Mexico City, Kearny's left arm was shattered by grapeshot while leading a charge. His arm was amputated in a makeshift field hospital as brigadier general (and future president) Franklin Pierce held his head. He was on his feet again within a very short time and was the first U.S. soldier to enter Mexico City after it fell to the Americans. General Scott called him "the bravest man I ever knew and a perfect soldier."

After Mexico, Kearny was brevetted to a major's rank and served in the Oregon Territory fighting Native Americans. Even so, peacetime service bored Kearny, and he resigned from the army to travel the world. He finally settled in New Jersey for a while with his mistress, then moved to Paris, where they were married in 1859. Back in France, he rejoined his old French comrades-in-arms and fought the Austrians in the Second Italian War for Independence. He served conspicuously at Magenta, and at the Battle of Solferino, he participated in a cavalry charge that helped break the Austrian army. For his gallantry, he was awarded the French Legion of Honor by Emperor Napoleon III.

When the Civil War broke out, the lure of more combat was too great, and Philip Kearny returned to the United States, where he was commissioned a brigadier general in the Union army. He trained the First New Jersey Brigade of the new Army of the Potomac and accompanied General George McClellan's army to the Virginia Peninsula in April 1862. There, he was made commander of the Third Division of the Army's III Corps.

Just a few days later, in the early-morning hours of May 5, 1862, Brigadier General Philip Kearny found himself on the Lee's Mill–Hampton Road in a heavy rain. He was pushing his new division toward the city of Williamsburg and the sound of battle. Farther up the very same road in front of him, Union brigadier general Joseph Hooker's division had been fighting the Confederates outside of Williamsburg for several hours and

*Right*: Major General Joseph Hooker. *National Archives.*

*Below*: Hooker's attack on the Confederates at Williamsburg as shown in *Harper's Weekly*, May 1862. *National Archives.*

were low on ammunition. Hooker's men would soon be overrun, and he needed help fast.

As Kearny led his troops up that muddy road, he met the confusion and disorder of the battle. With several wagons blocking the road, he ordered them to be moved, threatening to torch them himself if necessary. Meanwhile, the III Corps commander, General Samuel Heintzelman, had personally tried to rally Hooker's troops as they began to fall back to the rear. Riding among Hooker's retreating soldiers, Heintzelman ordered a Federal band sitting in a ditch to "Play Yankee Doodle, or any other damned doodle that you know!"

A dramatic view of Kearny's Brigade advancing in the rain at Williamsburg, May 5, 1862. *Library of Congress.*

It was at that critical moment in the battle that Kearny the Magnificent appeared. Seeing the chaos to his front, Kearny met some New Jersey troops that he had trained. Finding they had no officers and no orders, he cried to them, "Well, I am a one-armed Jersey son-of-gun! Follow me!" He then ordered his own men into a line of battle to bolster the wavering troops. So that his men could easily identify him, Kearny removed an India rubber cape that he had been wearing as protection from the rain. He stopped in front of one Michigan regiment and asked why they weren't advancing. Their colonel replied that they didn't know where the Confederates were. At that, Kearny spurred his horse forward, saying, "I'll show you!" His horse had trotted halfway across the field when gun smoke erupted from the woods to his front and bullets splattered around him. Now that he had exposed the Confederates, Kearny calmly rode back, shouting, "You see, my boys, where to fire!" He then yelled to his troops, "Men, I want you to drive those blackguards to hell at once!"

Although he had been their commander for a very short time, General Philip Kearny led his troops from the front that day in the rain at Williamsburg, and everyone in his division saw him in action with his sword in his right hand and the reins of his horse in his teeth. A New York officer with Hooker's Division later wrote:

*I saw Kearny come on the field...and of course had heard what a fierce fighter he was...but in all my days I never witnessed anything to equal what I saw him do...He rode in front of the enemy's lines, exposing himself so the Rebels would uncover their position.*

While he rode back and forth, always in front of his battle line, Kearny shouted, "Don't worry boys, they're shooting at me, not at you!" And the soldiers loved him, shouting, "Kearny! Kearny!" One private from Pennsylvania said it for all when he stated that Kearny "gave a hoot and holler about what was happening to us." As the battle wound down and darkness descended on the field, Kearny and his division had held the Union left flank and prevented a disaster.

In the next few days, Kearny entered Williamsburg and was invited by Rebecca Ewell to stay at the President's House at the College of William & Mary. Rebecca was the sister of the college's president, Benjamin Ewell, now a colonel in the retreating Southern army, and Confederate major general Richard Ewell. Kearney wrote to his wife, Agnes:

*My stay in Williamsburgh with Miss Ewell was most pleasant. She knew all about me, said that her brother, the General, my old comrade from Mexico, frequently spoke of me, and that in the Secession Army, that they all said, that I was bound to be a good officer.*

Kearny would remember Williamsburg as the place where he buried two of his staff officers "in a sweet spot, in the old 'Grave Yard' of Williamsburgh" and as a "lovely sweet College town of charming villas & old mansions."

But touring the town was not on Kearny's mind as he set about criticizing McClellan for not being on the field until the day's end and then giving all the credit to General Winfield Scott Hancock's troops fighting on the left of the Union battle line rather than his own. McClellan later issued an official apology and congratulated Kearny's division on their service at Williamsburg. This perceived slight, however, only further drove a wedge into the already strained relations between Kearny and his commander.

After the Union retreat from the Battle of Malvern Hill in July 1862, Kearny formally stated that McClellan was either a coward or a traitor. Kearny went on to lead his division in the Union defeat at the Second Battle of Manassas, and it was said that President Lincoln was considering him as his next choice to command the Army of the Potomac.

Tragically, Kearny's time had run out. After exposing himself to Confederate fire once too often, he was killed at the Battle of Chantilly on September 1, 1862, less than four months after saving that Union left flank on a muddy field at Williamsburg.

# SARAH EDMONDS

C aptain William Morse of the Second Michigan Volunteer Infantry had special reason to remember the fighting at Williamsburg on May 5, 1862. As his regiment went into the battle, Captain Morse had his feet knocked out from under him as he received a Confederate musket ball in his leg just below the knee. Fortunately for him, several members of his unit placed him on a stretcher and carried him several miles to the Federal hospital transport ship *Commodore*. The steamship carried Morse to Fort Monroe, where he was later transported to a hospital in Brooklyn, New York. Not known to Captain Morse was the fact that one of the men who had carried him to the transport landing was really a woman in disguise.

Sarah Emma Edmonds was born in New Brunswick, Canada, in 1841. After attempting to escape an arranged marriage (and apparently inspired by a book entitled *Fanny Campbell, the Female Pirate Captain*), Edmonds cut her curly hair and assumed the name Franklin Thompson. Posing as a young boy, Edmonds became a successful traveling salesman of religious books and found herself in Michigan when the Civil War broke out. On April 17, 1861, "Franklin Thompson" enlisted in the Flint Union Greys, which became Company F of the Second Michigan Infantry. The regiment left for Washington, where Private Thompson worked as a male nurse in the brigade hospital. At the Battle of Manassas in July 1861, Thompson served at a field hospital and was almost captured by the victorious Confederates.

The next March, Thompson's regiment was sent to Fort Monroe in Virginia as part of General George B. McClellan's campaign against

Richmond. Initially, Franklin Thompson was made regimental mail carrier, but a chaplain recommended Frank for a special assignment. Edmonds, still disguised as Frank, was interviewed and became a spy for General McClellan. After shaving her head, Emma adopted a disguise as a Negro laborer and crossed over into the Rebel lines around Yorktown. Upon returning with information about Confederate troop strength, Private Thompson rejoined the Second Michigan.

On May 5, 1862, only about sixty members of the Second Michigan were present on the battlefield at Williamsburg as part of General Philip Kearny's division, but Edmonds was among them. Besides Captain Morse, eleven other members of the regiment became casualties that day. After carrying the captain off the field, she helped where she could. She spent the long night after the battle in a makeshift hospital assisting the surgeons with their work.

Sarah Edmonds. *Library and Archives Canada.*

During her brief stay in Williamsburg over the next few days, Edmonds procured the disguise of an Irish female peddler. As the Federal army slowly made its way toward Richmond over the next few weeks, she once again crossed over into Confederate territory to spy for General McClellan.

Franklin Thompson continued to serve with the Second Michigan until the spring of 1863, when the regiment was in Kentucky. Taken ill with a malarial fever, Edmonds deserted the army rather than entering a hospital and risk being found out. She reassumed her female identity, and in 1864, she published a book, *Nurse and Spy*, that detailed her adventures. She dedicated the book "to the sick and wounded soldiers of the Army of Potomac," and the proceeds from the book were donated to the U.S. Sanitary and Christian Commissions to help them in their efforts to comfort Union soldiers.

After the war, Sarah Edmonds married Linus H. Seelye and worked for the Freedmen's Bureau in the South, helping to educate newly freed slaves. For her wartime service as a nurse and her devotion to her comrades on the battlefield, she received a pension from Congress of twelve dollars per month. In 1897, she was accepted into the Union veterans' organization, the Grand Army of the Republic—the only woman ever to be so honored.

Highly respected for her service to her country, Sarah Edmonds died the next year in Laporte, Texas. The young woman who had carried her captain off the battlefield at Williamsburg many years before was finally laid to rest at a special Memorial Day service in Houston.

# THE DEAD AND WOUNDED

The battle that occurred outside of Williamsburg on May 5, 1862, was considered a delaying action, as Confederate general Joseph E. Johnston merely wished to hold off the Union advance until his supply train and the bulk of his army had made it down the road toward Richmond. Compared to later Civil War battles, it would not seem significant. But to the men who were killed and wounded, Williamsburg was just as deadly a battle as Gettysburg or Chickamauga.

The Battle of Williamsburg claimed the lives of almost four thousand Union and Confederate soldiers. The fields and woods around the town were filled with the dead and wounded. The city itself became a field hospital in the days following the battle. As it dealt with the combination of the effects of the battle and the Federal occupation that lasted more than three years after it, Williamsburg would never be the same.

Colonel William Kreutzer of the Ninety-Eighth New York Infantry wrote about the scene just outside the town. Although his men had not been in the battle itself, as they came up from Yorktown on May 6, they furnished burial details to begin the cleanup of the human devastation:

> Our road crossed a tributary of Queen's Creek, on the head of a mill-dam, and passing through an evacuated redoubt, ran over the field on which Hancock made his brilliant advance the evening before. Two or three hundred of the enemy's dead still lay where they fell. His wounded were collected in a barn a shed near the battle-ground. Arriving at Fort Magruder, the division sent details to bury the dead down the Williamsburg road.

A view of a barn being used as a hospital after the Battle of Williamsburg. *National Archives.*

While the burial parties were at work, Kreutzer walked the battlefield with two or three other officers. He noted how the Confederates had cut trees on both sides of the road to create a tangled obstacle for the advancing Union troops. Here, he noted that there must have been fierce fighting:

*There, the wounded, the dying were thickest. On the brush, among the limbs, against the stumps and trunks, in the mud, in the water, on the wet ground, they lay. In the road, along the road, in the grass, on the leaves, in the slashing, in the ditches, cold and dead they lay, a heart-rending commentary on a nation's quarrel.*

In the city itself, Union captain Henry Blake recorded his impressions of Williamsburg the day after the battle:

*All the desolations of war, the legitimate results of the Rebellion, were visible throughout it limits; and the public buildings, halls, churches, and many dwelling houses were filled with the wounded of both armies. The yellow flags, which indicated the rebel hospitals—red was the color of the Union hospital flag—waved in every district.*

Although the women of Williamsburg were taken aback by the occupation of their town, they responded to the desperate needs of the wounded. According to Cynthia B.T. Coleman:

*They rouse themselves...remembering that duty lies before them, for even now the hospitals and Churches occupied by wounded soldiers who are alike prisoners of war, needing the ministering care and sympathy of woman. Soon are seen groups of two and threes with baskets in hand and faces closely veiled winding their way to the Episcopal and other Churches where war reveals its horrors to those who here see for the first time death and wounds accompanied with the heroic fortitude of the true soldier. In the Chancel lay a magnificent form from which the spirit had fled. A wounded comrade with quivering lip said, "He is dead Madam;" in the aisles are three or four more of the dead mingled with the living.*

In Williamsburg Baptist Church, Confederate surgeons were overwhelmed by the number of wounded but continued their grisly work. Women visiting the church-turned-hospital personally discovered the horrors of war. One woman unexpectedly discovered an amputation in progress, which she termed "a shocking operation." Years later, Victoria Lee, the young refugee from Hampton, remembered:

*This building was used as a hospital, and at times I helped to care for the soldiers brought there. One morning, a few days after the Battle of Williamsburg, I entered the basement door of this building—I was carrying a pitcher of buttermilk to the sick soldiers—and, as I stepped through the doorway, one of the most horrible sights I have ever seen met my eyes—in a corner of the basement room was a pile of human arms and legs.*

Many wounded Confederates found themselves taken into private homes by the inhabitants of the town. In the dark and rainy night that followed the battle, Lieutenant Charles S. Fleming of the Second Florida was carried off the field by his brother, Francis. Unable to find an ambulance, Francis gathered volunteers from a passing Virginia regiment and managed to move Lieutenant Fleming into the town, where they stopped at a large, lit-up house on Waller Street. This was the home of a widow named Mary Claiborne. A number of wounded had already been collected in her front yard under the care of an Alabama surgeon. At

Captain Charles Seton Fleming.
From *Memoir of Capt. C. Seton
Fleming, of the Second Florida Infantry,
C.S.A.* (published in 1884), by
Francis Fleming. *Author's collection.*

daylight, Francis left his brother with Claiborne and rejoined his regiment. Charles Fleming later wrote to his father and mother:

> *I was wounded by a rifle or musket-ball which entered the center of my right side, about an inch above my hip-bone, and came out alongside of my backbone. I suppose that Frank wrote you that he left me at a private house, where I was taken about three o'clock that night. The Yankees, who came in town next morning, did not have me removed to a hospital but let me remain at the same house; where I was, indeed very lucky to get, for the lady who staid there was just as kind and attentive to me as though I were her own and only child. There was nothing that I wanted that was not gotten for me, if it could be had in town. I was confined to bed for about seven weeks, during which time I suffered more from fever than the actual pain that my wound occasioned. The people of Williamsburg are as patriotic as they can be—the ladies especially.*

Emily Morrison, who lived with her mother next to the hospital at the Williamsburg Female Academy, also took in a wounded Confederate soldier, Private William J. Davis of the Eighteenth Virginia Infantry. Davis was a young man from Prince Edward County who had enlisted in April 1861 in the Prospect Rifle Grays. During the battle outside town, he had been wounded in both legs and was being nursed by "Miss Emily." Despite her efforts, Private Davis took a turn for the worse. He was removed by the Federal authorities to the hospital at the Williamsburg Baptist Church.

Postwar view of the Williamsburg Baptist Church. It served as a hospital during the 1862 battle outside of town. *Special Collections, John D. Rockefeller Jr. Library, Colonial Williamsburg Foundation.*

There, his right leg was amputated, and he died in the hospital in early June. Cynthia Coleman wrote:

> *Little Davis is dead, poor young boy far from home and mother to lay down his life. He has found in Miss Emily a faithful tender nurse. The whole Confederate heart of the town is filled with pity for the poor lad who having lost one leg has now lost his life.*

Several ladies of Williamsburg accompanied his body to the city cemetery, where he was placed in a shallow grave. "Miss Emily," heartbroken, was present at the burial as one of the mourners.

Cynthia Coleman recorded another incident that occurred at the Baptist church hospital during the early days of the Federal occupation:

> *This morning while going my rounds somebody shouted "They are going to blow up the Hospital." Such excitement I never saw. The poor bed-*

*ridden wounded unable to move filled with alarm, the women flying about like crazy people, nobody seeming to know exactly what was the matter. I finally discovered that a train of powder had been laid along the passage to reach a keg of powder concealed in a closet by old clothing cut from the wounded, and thrown aside with the bloody rags used in dressing their wounds. These things alone saved the building, for when I reached the spot almost paralyzed with terror, I had just sense enough left to drag them down upon the train of powder, at the other end of which the fuse was sputtering. The guard could nowhere be found. When the attention of the Officer of the day was called to the outrage, he pretended not to believe it, or to know who was on guard. The only conclusion that I can come to is, that the Officers are afraid to punish their men, and, no wonder, for they are fiends in human form.*

On the west end of town, there occurred an especially poignant scene that was later described by Cynthia Coleman:

*One young Confederate, mortally wounded, was taken to the Ware house, in which then lived old Mrs. Elizabeth Ware and her married daughter. This soldier boy died soon after reaching this house. He was tenderly cared for and placed in the parlor of this home awaiting disposition of the body. When General McClellan took possession of this city, the day after the battle....A Union soldier presented himself at the door of his house and, as instructed, asked if there were any sick or wounded soldiers there. When informed that there was a dead soldier there, he walked into the parlor and upon removing the sheet that covered the face of the corpse, the sorrowful fact was revealed that the live Union soldier was the brother of the dead Confederate lad; and as those kind-hearted southern women stood about the room, their eyes filled with tears for they knew the deceased was some Mother's darling and while they wept a tragic scene was enacted as the soldier in blue knelt by the bier and implanted a kiss on the brow of his dead brother, clad in Confederate gray. Soon an ambulance arrived, the corpse was placed therein and driven away—thus grimly demonstrating the truth of the expressions so often heard that this War was one of "Father against son, brother against brother."*

Determined to aid the suffering soldiers who were now prisoners of war, Letitia Tyler Semple, who had organized the hospital at the Williamsburg Female Academy, remained defiant even after she found herself behind

Federal lines. Cynthia Coleman accompanied Semple as she visited the Confederate wounded at Bruton Parish Church just after the Battle of Williamsburg and the arrival of Union troops into the city:

> *A friend* [Letitia Semple]…*called on me to accompany her. To reach the Episcopal Church we were obliged to cross the Palace Green filled…with Federal Cavalry. They took no notice of us nor we of them. I shall never forget the scene of horror that met my eye when I entered that Church.*

Inside, the two women found the wounded and dead everywhere, even within the chancel railing. Boards had been laid over pews to hold men as they were waiting for care, and the air was filled with constant moans and crying. Union medical staff were in the church attempting to help as much as possible, but like the rest of the town, they were overwhelmed. One such soldier left an unfavorable impression on the staunchly Confederate Cynthia Coleman:

> *With the dead and dying all around us a sniveling, fawning fellow in Federal uniform came up, whining, "This is a very distressing scene, ladies."*
> *"Yes, it is," was the curt reply of my friend, Mrs. S.*
> *"It gave me great pain to decide to take up arms against our people," continued the whiner.*
> *"Our people, what do you mean by that?" queried Mrs. S.*
> *"Oh! I am a Southern man."*
> *"You are," in tones that should have annihilated him, "never let me hear you speak again of our people, but you have only followed the example of Cain who killed his brother Abel."*
> *He slunk away and we did not see him again.*

After the town was occupied, Confederate surgeon J.S.D. Cullen, medical director of the army's Second Division, and at least ten other regimental surgeons and volunteer doctors returned to Williamsburg to help tend to the wounded. They were first taken up as prisoners by the Federals but then released because of their noncombatant status. William W. Potter, assistant surgeon to the Forty-Ninth New York Infantry, offered his observations on his Confederate counterparts and the wounded left behind:

*The wounded in Williamsburg—400 or 500—were left there in care of the rebel surgeons, who were sent into our lines for that purpose. Some of these doctors were quite intelligent looking men, but most of them were shabbily dressed and were only to be distinguished from civilians by the letters "M.S."—signifying medical staff—on their hats. Williamsburg itself is a sleepy old village of probably 2,000 inhabitants in time of peace. Many of them had now retired with the rebel army.*

Another Federal surgeon, Alfred Hitchcock, reported to his superiors concerning the wounded at the college:

*I was at once placed in charge as Senior Surgeon of the College Hospital. Dr. Bronson and two Confederate surgeons have assisted me. Mr. Wellman has kept the records and assisted in the dressings. My record yesterday morning made up 275 Union patients and 80 Rebels—about one half of them we sent to Fort Monroe yesterday—and last night we received 50 more.*

A newspaper woodcut of "The Old Episcopal Burial Ground" at Bruton Parish Church. *Special Collections, John D. Rockefeller Jr. Library, Colonial Williamsburg Foundation.*

Finally, James J. Marks, a clergyman serving with the Federal army, described his own impressions of the newly occupied town of Williamsburg after a visit to Bruton Parish Church:

*Amongst the most interesting monuments of the past, I found the old English church, where lie entombed many of the early governors, judges, and military captains who lived and died prior to the Revolution. This church had been occupied as a hospital; the seats torn up, and beds, cots, and stretchers extended over the whole building; and across the floor in every direction had run streams of blood. Into this had been gathered, after the battle of Williamsburg, great numbers of the wounded and dying of the rebel army: outside of the church, on the grounds amidst the monuments and tents, the wounded had all been placed, and every spot was baptized with blood, and even on the white slabs were the traces of human suffering.*

# The Unknown Horse

One of the lesser known sorrows of the Civil War was the fact that more than one million horses and mules died during the conflict. These forgotten participants were present at almost every skirmish, raid and battle of the war, and because of their importance to both sides, they became just as targeted as any soldier on the field.

By far, the largest users of horses and mules were the quartermasters, with their supply wagons and ambulances. Hundreds of thousands of animals were needed to carry food, supplies and the wounded. In theory, a single Federal infantry division of three brigades required a minimum of two thousand horses and mules, not counting reserve replacement animals. Added to that number were the horses and mules needed just to carry the fodder for the animals that were carrying supplies for the troops.

Then, there was that great user of horseflesh, the cavalry. Not only did every trooper require a mount, but there needed to be countless remounts. Horses and mules were essential for the artillery; they were not only used for pulling the many cannons but also for the forge wagons and ammunition caissons. Sadly, it was a common tactic on the battlefield to shoot at artillery horses in order to immobilize an artillery battery.

Finally, there were the mounted generals and other assorted officers, staff and couriers. One can quickly see that there were an awful lot of horses on and around any given Civil War battlefield.

We remember the famous horses of the war, such as General Lee's Traveller, Stonewall Jackson's Little Sorrel or General Grant's Cincinnati,

Archaeological examination of a horse burial that took place during the fighting around Williamsburg. *Colonial Williamsburg Foundation.*

but unfortunately, the great majority of equines that served in the war remain unknown and unremembered.

One such unknown creature, typical of the many horses lost, was found in Williamsburg by Colonial Williamsburg archaeologists more than 130 years after the war ended. Discovered in a ditch near the Anthony Hay Shop on Nicholson Street, the animal's remains were observed to be a Civil War burial. The skeleton revealed that it was a male horse, approximately five years old. The animal had been shot twice—once in the flank, where a lead Minié ball was found, and secondly, in the head, where a round lead ball was located. Buried in a shallow grave, its legs had been hacked, possibly with an axe. The simplest explanation is that sometime during the war, either in the 1862 Battle of Williamsburg or in one of the numerous skirmishes in the area, the horse became one of the war's victims. It had been shot in the flank by either a Union or Confederate rifled musket. The animal was later apparently put out of its misery with a gunshot to the head. The method of burial seems to have been standard practice for either side; the animal's legs were broken to fit it into a quickly dug shallow grave.

We shall never know the poor horse's name or on which side he served, but like the many soldiers on both sides who died in and around Williamsburg during the war, he was also part of the tragedy.

# THE CONFEDERATE GENERALS

It is interesting to note that on the Confederate side, seven generals or future generals were among the wounded on the Williamsburg battlefield on May 5, 1862.

Brigadier General Jubal Early was wounded twice as he led his men in an attack on the Union right. Early's brigade had been called forward late in the day to check a threat posed by the troops of Union general Winfield Scott Hancock. In much pain and weak from loss of blood, Early had to leave the field and was taken to a hospital in Williamsburg. There, it was discovered that a rifle ball had entered one shoulder and passed around his back to the other shoulder.

After he was treated in the town, General Early was evacuated with other Confederate wounded as the Southern army left the town on the night of the battle. He returned to the army several months later but was in poor health for the rest of the war. After being promoted to lieutenant general, he commanded a Confederate army in the Shenandoah Valley in 1864 that threatened Washington, D.C., before being defeated. Early ended the war debilitated with rheumatism.

As a captain in the Tenth Alabama Infantry, William Henry Forney had his right arm fractured by a bullet. After he was taken to the hospital at the College of William & Mary, medical personnel discovered that his wound was too serious for him to be removed. Captain Forney found himself a prisoner of war when Federal troops occupied the city the next day. He eventually recovered from his wound and was shipped through Fort Monroe in Hampton to captivity in the North. After being freed through a prisoner exchange, he was wounded and captured a second time at Gettysburg. After being exchanged once again, Forney ended the war as a brigadier general at Appomattox.

Colonel Samuel Garland Jr. of the Eleventh Virginia Infantry was wounded in the elbow by a musket ball. Not considering his wound to be serious, Garland refused to leave the field to be treated and continued fighting with his regiment. After retreating toward Richmond with his command, he was promoted to brigadier general in May. Garland was killed in September 1862 while holding off a Federal attack at Fox's Gap at South Mountain.

Confederate brigadier general Jubal Early. *Brady-Handy Collection, Library of Congress.*

Like Colonel Garland, Captain Nathaniel H. Harris of the Nineteenth Mississippi Infantry was only slightly wounded at Williamsburg and continued fighting throughout the day, leaving the field with his men. He received a second, more serious wound, however, outside of Richmond at the Battle of Frayser's Farm less than two months later. He received a third wound at the Battle of Second Manassas in August 1862. Harris ended the war as a brigadier general.

Major William H.F. Payne of the Fourth Virginia Cavalry was seriously wounded in the mouth and fell from his horse while observing the Battle of Williamsburg from near one of the Confederate redoubts. Dr. E.S. Pendleton immediately stopped the flow of blood from Payne's face by holding his hand on the wound. After being carried back into Williamsburg in a military ambulance with Dr. Pendleton still holding the wound, Payne was taken to the house of William Peachy on the Market Square. Today, visitors touring the same house learn that it was the home of Peyton Randolph, speaker of the House of Burgesses and first president of the Continental Congress.

After being captured the next day by the advancing Federal army, Payne was fortunately allowed to remain in Peachy's house because of the serious nature of his wound. With his jaw badly damaged, he had to be fed through

*Left*: Confederate brigadier general Samuel Garland. *Library of Congress*.

*Right*: Confederate brigadier general William H.F. Payne. *Library of Congress*.

a flexible tube, and his wound healed slowly. It was through the intervention of his wife, Mary, that Major Payne obtained his freedom. Although she was a refugee and pregnant at the time, Mary Payne journeyed to Williamsburg from Danville, Virginia, to personally treat her husband. After a circuitous trip that took her to Richmond, Alexandria, Baltimore and, finally, Hampton, she arrived in Williamsburg and located her husband. Once in the city, she procured a parole for the wounded officer to return to his home in Warrenton, Virginia.

After only partially recovering, Payne rejoined the army as Lee headed toward Pennsylvania in 1863. He was wounded and captured a second time at Hanover, Pennsylvania, on June 30, 1863, during the Gettysburg Campaign. He passed another year in a prisoner-of-war camp before he was exchanged. In November 1864, Payne was appointed a brigadier general of cavalry. On March 30, 1865, he received a last wound near Five Forks, Virginia. Avoiding the surrender of General Lee's army at Appomattox, he was captured on the night of President Lincoln's assassination. General Payne remained a Federal prisoner until May, when he finally returned to his home and family at Warrenton.

Also wounded in the face, Colonel William R. Terry fell leading the Twenty-Fourth Virginia Infantry in the same charge in which General

*Left*: Confederate brigadier general William Terry. *Library of Congress.*

*Right*: Confederate brigadier general Zebulon York. *Library of Congress.*

Early got his wound. Apparently, Terry's wound was not as serious as Major Payne's, for Terry did not seem to stay long under a surgeon's care. Continuing with the army, he was promoted to the rank of brigadier general in May 1864. General Terry was reportedly wounded a total of seven times during the war, including at Pickett's Charge at Gettysburg and when he received a broken leg due to a shell burst that killed his horse at Dinwiddie Court House in March 1865.

Although born in Maine, Lieutenant Colonel Zebulon York was with the Fourteenth Louisiana Infantry when he received a slight wound at Williamsburg. He left with the Confederate retreat and remained with the army during the Seven Days Battles around Richmond. Promoted to brigadier general in May 1864, York was wounded a second time and had an arm amputated at the Battle of Winchester on September 19 of that year. Even with the loss of his arm, York continued his service to the Confederacy. He ended the war on recruiting duty.

Finally, an eighth officer who would serve both as a Confederate general and a congressman was present in Williamsburg during the battle, although he had been wounded the day before. In a cavalry skirmish on the evening of May 4, 1862, Lieutenant Colonel Williams Carter Wickham was involved in a charge in which he received a saber cut in his side. Although seriously wounded, he continued to fight. The next day, he left with the army, moving toward Richmond. He was captured while recovering from the saber slash at his father's house in Ashland, Virginia. Paroled and exchanged, Colonel Wickham was promoted to brigadier general in September 1863. He resigned his commission a year later to take a seat in the Confederate Congress.

Although these eight men were only a few of the thousands who had reason to remember Williamsburg, they were each a part of the town's darkest hours.

# OCCUPATION AND POLITE RESISTANCE

O n May 6, 1862, Williamsburg became an occupied town. The morning after the battle, General Stoneman's Federal cavalry cautiously entered the city from the east. Determining that Williamsburg was undefended, General McClellan secured the town before renewing his pursuit of the retreating Rebels. Once again, the streets of Williamsburg were filled with marching soldiers, but this time, they were dressed in Union blue. Speaking of the arrival of the Union army, one resident remembered:

> *McClellan's Army followed close on the heels of Johnston's. It was one of the most magnificent sights I have ever seen—countless thousands of blue-clad troops, all in new uniforms, they were several days passing through Williamsburg. I saw part of this army when it returned from the vicinity of Richmond—it didn't look so splendid then.*

With the arrival of "the enemy," life changed in the city. The last year had been spent in the exhilaration of a new nation; now, Williamsburg was occupied by what the inhabitants considered to be a foreign army. In a diary, Williamsburg resident Harriette Cary recorded her impressions of the first few days of Federal occupation:

> *May 6, 1862…General McClellan's Army took possession this morning about nine o'clock. It seems finely organized and most splendidly equipped—the men robust and well uniformed—especially the officers,*

Company C, Sixth Maine Infantry. These men fought at Williamsburg in May 1862 and later marched through the town on the road to Richmond. *Library of Congress.*

*yet the utter detestation with which I regard these vandals engenders a disgust which I would not feel for the vilest man on our Southern Soil. A representative of General McClellan's Staff has applied for rooms, but was refused. A fine looking officer with two men very respectfully announced this morning their orders to search, which was but <u>nominal</u>—a glance at each room seemed only necessary—all houses were subjected to the same with more or less scrutiny...General McClellan is a neighbor of ours—has taken possession of Dr. Vest's house occupied by Gen. Johnston C.S.A. yesterday....All is quiet and being assured of protection by two Sentinels placed at our door I shall seek repose, first asking God's blessing on my dear relatives and friends. My heart is sad! God be with the absent ones!*

*May 7th.—The Federal army is still moving and seems exhaustless.... Various rumors I have caught from soldiers passing by—Richmond is taken—Magruder captured with 12,000 men—both of which I believe to be Yankee lies...The familiar tune of Dixie I heard this evening—at rather a distance however, from which I located the Band at College. Yankee ingenuity—I believe is indefatigable—Artillery, infantry and cavalry going up and coming down incessantly.... To the Omnipotent I commit the keeping of our dear soldiers!*

Amid the anguish of the town being occupied by Federal troops, young John Charles recalled an amusing incident that occurred on the east end of town at a dwelling known as the Frog Pond Tavern. It drew its name from a large mud hole in the Stage Road that "produced fine crops of frogs that furnished entertainment for the Tavern guests and to the neighbors during the summer months." He wrote:

*At the beginning of hostilities this Tavern was owned by an old gentleman, who was familiarly called "Old By Jucks."...He ran a store where both solid and liquid refreshments were served; and in connection with the store there was a large stable yard, where on court day and other occasions, the farmers' vehicles were put, and where their horses were fed.... Old By Jucks was a kind-hearted and genial old fellow, and tradition has it that on the morning of the most sorrowful day in old Williamsburg's history, May 6th, 1862, when McClellan's great army entered this city, Old Jucks, highly excited and greatly alarmed, as everyone else was, went out in front*

A watercolor of Union wagons and troops passing through Williamsburg on May 9, 1862. *Library of Congress.*

*of his house, from the porch of which hung a white flag; and with hat in hand made a polite bow to the advance guard of McClellan's vast army, and exclaimed, "Good morning, gentlemen, come in and have some hot biscuits and coffee."*

At first, there was great fear for personal safety. General McClellan had issued orders that private property was to be respected and safeguarded, but this did not allay the apprehensions of many. Cynthia Coleman remembered:

*At our front gate stood a sentinel placed there by order of McClellan to protect us in our homes, though we did not understand that at the time. I shall never forget his appearance or how I hated him. In a little time the beautiful Court House Green in front of my Mother's house was filled with their army wagon's, horses and soldiers....The houses abandoned by their owners were speedily converted into barracks, the Churches with Hospitals for the wounded of our Army. The Town was full. Anxious hearts beat that day in women's breasts.*

Of course, the occupying army had its own opinion of Williamsburg and its residents. One Union soldier wrote of the inhabitants he encountered:

*The people, with few exceptions, were traitors who had always encouraged those that murdered the forces that upheld the National Government; and the closed and empty stores, the absence of the able-bodied white men, the scowls of the women and children, and the delighted faces of the Negroes were perceived by the most casual observer.*

Generally, during the three and a half years when Federal forces occupied Williamsburg, the white female residents of Williamsburg refused to give any willing assistance to their conquerors. Although they were not as contentious as the ladies of occupied New Orleans, who spat on Federal officers, the ladies of Williamsburg did offer passive resistance whenever possible. On the main street, they refused to walk under the U.S. flag. Victoria King wrote:

*The United States troops who were left in Williamsburg after McClellan passed through on the way to Richmond, used this building as a commissary. A large flag—a United States flag, of course—was placed on the front of this building, so that it hung out over the sidewalk; and the girls of Williamsburg, to avoid walking under it, used to walk out in the road.*

*The United States troops, not to be outdone, however, got a long flag and stretched it completely across the Main Street.*

A Federal military newspaper published in Williamsburg, the *Cavalier,* offered an account of one young woman who requested that a photographer take a picture of her trampling a U.S. flag under her feet:

*The reply of the artist was very proper and the rebuke merited: "I will grant your modest request, provided you will grant me a favor."*

*"What is it, sir? I will do anything reasonable you may request so that I can have the picture taken."*

*"Oh! Miss, it is very simple and easily done. All I require of you is to elevate your pedal extremities toward heaven, and stand on your head on the 'Stars and Stripes,' and then I will take your likeness."*

The *Cavalier,* printed by Union cavalrymen, had begun publication notwithstanding the efforts of Mary Lively, the mother of two of Williamsburg's more literary minded young men, Robert and Edward Lively.

Edward was the publisher and Robert was the printer of the *Eastern Virginia Advertiser and Weekly Gazette.* This newspaper traced its lineage back to the 1730s (as the *Virginia Gazette*), and in 1860, it was the only paper published between Richmond and Norfolk. The paper was printed in Mary Lively's basement on the western end of the Duke of Gloucester Street near the College of William & Mary. It was the *Eastern Virginia Advertiser and Weekly Gazette* that urged the formation of a local militia unit—"the Williamsburg Junior Guard"—after John Brown's raid at Harper's Ferry in October 1859.

With Edward's marriage in late 1860 and the coming of war, the paper ceased publication. As Virginia left the Union in 1861, Edward raised a secessionist flag over his mother's house, and both brothers enlisted in the Confederate cause and marched off to war.

Meanwhile, the idle presses remained in Mary Lively's basement. With the Union occupation of the town, they became of great interest to members of the Fifth Pennsylvania Cavalry. On June 25, 1862, the Pennsylvanians began publication of their own newspaper utilizing the presses and equipment located in Mary's basement. An article in the *Richmond Dispatch* titled "Peninsula Items, February 25th, 1863" tells us something of the tribulations of Mary Lively:

*The following paragraphs are the products of a peep at odd times, within the past few weeks, into the Yankee lines behind Yankee scouts and Yankee pickets, by a rebel scout...The press, material, etc, of the* Williamsburg Gazette *office was demanded a few weeks since by General Keys for the use of the United States forces at Yorktown. The importunities of Mrs. Lively, the mother of the editor of the* Gazette, *who retreated with our army in May last, had no effect. The Lieut. of the guard ordered the men to break the office door down unless she, Mrs. L, would give up the keys. Being alarmed by this and other similar threats, Mrs. Lively had to surrender the keys. The press, etc, was taken off to Yorktown where the publication of the Yankee* Cavalier *sheet is continued. This dirty sheet was lies, printed in the* Gazette *office.*

The defiance of the women in Williamsburg was the subject of an editorial in the *Cavalier* printed under the heading "Local Items" in the first issue on June 25, 1862:

*A SIGN OF CHIVALRY---We notice a new and peculiar trait of character in this community for which we are at a loss for a name, and which, for convenience, we will call "gratitude." It is most conspicuous in those who are in part or entirely dependent on the generosity of the good old United States, and its officers in this place, for their peace, safety, and in some instances, their daily bread. It shows itself in a strained and bombastic effort to insult, in every conceivable way, the soldiers and officers of our regiment, and what is more infamous still, the glorious old flag of the Union, which is dear to every heart free from treason. We have seen the supercilious flirt, with scarcely enough sense to avoid running into the fire, with upturned, bloodshot eyes, and protruding tongue, as she approached the place where our banner was proudly floating, exclaimed to a companion: "Oh! mercy! See what we wer 'goin'ty trodden under," and then, self-conscious that she was unfit to go near, though pretending to be horrified at its sight, she gently stepped off of the beautiful sidewalk, her fairy foot lightly pressing the mud six inches deep....We were much affected by the touching scene, and sadly wandered away whistling "Yankee Doodle."*

No amount of editorializing could change the feelings of the Confederate inhabitants, however. When accosted by a Union soldier, one young lady was told, "Miss, I believe your hatred of Yankees is so great that you would not wish to see us in Heaven."

"Oh! Yes, I would," she replied, "for then you would be so changed I should not know you to be Yankees."

# SALLIE GALT

A personal tragedy that affected the entire Williamsburg community occurred during the first days of Federal occupation. The Galt family had been in the old colonial capital since the mid-eighteenth century, and three generations had served the Eastern State Lunatic Asylum as physicians.

Dr. John Minson Galt, the first member of the Galt family associated with the hospital, had been educated at the College of William & Mary and received his medical training both in Edinburgh and Paris. He became a prominent member of the Williamsburg community and served on the board of visitors of the college and, with the coming of the Revolutionary War, on the local committee of safety. He later served as an army surgeon, and during the siege of Yorktown in 1781, he was the senior field surgeon for General Washington. In 1791, Galt was appointed attending physician for the insane at the public hospital that had opened in Williamsburg seventeen years earlier.

When John Minson Galt died in 1808, his son, Dr. Alexander Dickie Galt, assumed his position. After Alexander married his cousin Maria (known as Mary) Dorothea Galt in 1812, they had four children: John Minson II, Alexander Jr., Elizabeth Judith and, finally, Sarah Maria, who was born on February 27, 1822. The family lived in the east end of Williamsburg, on Francis Street, until 1841, when Alexander died. His oldest son, now Dr. John Minson Galt II, took over his father's duties as the superintendent at the newly named Eastern State Lunatic Asylum.

Sarah Maria Galt, known as "Miss Sallie" (or Sally), grew up in a very close family and received an excellent education. The family was prominent

Dr. John Minson Galt II, superintendent of the Lunatic Asylum when Federal troops took control of Williamsburg. *Illustration from* The original 13 members of the Association of Medical Superintendents of American Institutions for the Insane *by John Curwen (1885).*

in Williamsburg, and throughout the 1840s and early 1850s, their house was filled with social gatherings and parties, but none of the four children ever married.

Sallie's life changed during the 1850s. Her brother Alexander Jr. had died in his twenties. Her only sister, Elizabeth (or Lizzie), died in 1854 after a long illness and years as an invalid. Finally, her mother, Mary, died in 1858, and Sallie was left alone with her brother John Minson Galt II, who was the superintendent of the asylum. She devoted herself to caring for him and took up residence with him in the superintendent's cottage at the hospital.

With the coming of war in 1861, Williamsburg became a city full of uniforms. Throughout the summer and fall, as newly formed companies of soldiers converged on Williamsburg from all over Virginia and the Deep South, Sallie became an ardent Confederate. She noted the arrival of the young volunteers:

*We have had the houses full of our officers & have taken the College & Courthouse for barracks. For the last few days many thousand soldiers have been in Wmsburg on their way to York Town & the region round about Hampton. A more gallant set of men never lived. They say they will fight all the more bravely for the unbounded hospitality of (the) ladies of Williamsburg.*

Sallie was especially proud to honor a request from General John Bankhead Magruder, commander of the Confederate forces at Yorktown. Although the area had been occupied by Virginians for over 250 years, there were no reliably detailed maps. General Magruder asked for the loan of a map of Yorktown that had belonged to her grandfather when he had served there in 1781 with George Washington's army, and she was "thankful we had it to lend him."

On May 5, 1862, with the Battle of Williamsburg and the subsequent occupation of the town, Sallie's life changed once again. The day after the arrival of Union troops, the Federal authorities denied her brother John entry into the asylum. The upheaval of his life and his inability to even visit the asylum inmates he had cared for broke Galt. Within just two weeks, he was dead from an overdose of laudanum. Sallie composed the obituary for her beloved brother, attempting to hide his apparent suicide:

> *In Memoriam. Died, in Williamsburg, Va., May 18th, 1862, after an illness of four days, of an affection of the stomach, to which he had been subject for many years, and which, reflecting on the brain, caused apoplexy, John M. Galt, M.D., son of the late Dr. Alexander D. Galt. Dr. Galt was Superintendent and Physician of the Eastern Lunatic Asylum at Williamsburg, Va., and he nobly and conscientiously performed the duties devolving upon him.*

With the death of her brother, Sallie was ordered by the Federal provost marshal to leave the superintendent's house that had become her home. She returned to the family house on the east side of Williamsburg in the company of two faithful slaves and a friend. Her grief was overpowering:

> *Pity my wretchedness. My darling brother was...all the world to me, & without him life to me is dark & dreary. I who have lived all my life in an atmosphere of love, now have no one to love, or to love me.*

In early 1864, Sallie faced a new dilemma. The Union commander of the local military district ordered that the citizens of Williamsburg must swear an oath of allegiance to the Federal government or depart the town. The oath required to be signed read:

> *I _____ do solemnly swear, in the presence of Almighty God, that I will bear true allegiance to the United States of America, and will obey and maintain the Constitution and the laws of the same, and will defend and support the said United States of America, against all enemies, foreign and domestic, and especially against the Rebellious league known as the Confederate States of America, So help me God.*

Sallie Galt's family home in Williamsburg. *Special Collections, John D. Rockefeller Jr. Library, Colonial Williamsburg Foundation.*

Rather than betray her Confederate beliefs, Sallie Galt petitioned a family friend, Dorothea Dix, for help. Dix was well known as a nurse and hospital reformer who, before the war, had crusaded for humane care for the mentally ill. Through her work, she was well acquainted with the Galt family and their contributions to the Eastern State Lunatic Asylum. By 1864, Dix had been appointed by President Lincoln as the Federal superintendent of female nurses. As such, she was frequently in the field around Fort Monroe and often visited Williamsburg. Sallie wrote to Dix:

> *You told me when you visited me in the summer, that anything you could do for me, you would…now I beseech you to help me with your influence with regard to the oath. It would almost make me crazy to take any oath to any government even General Washington's Government if he was living I could not promise to support….You are such an Angel of consolation & surely you will do something for me & have my sentence commuted as regards the oath. Don't tell me you have not the power for you can do anything you try.*

Dix personally spoke with General Benjamin Butler regarding the matter. There was no definite resolution to the issue, but with Dix's intervention, Sallie's taking of the oath was delayed by authorities. In appreciation for

Dorothea Lynde Dix. *Library of Congress.*

Dix's kindness, Sallie presented her with a part of a set of curtains that had been given to her grandfather by the Marquis de Lafayette in 1781:

> *Some vehement Confederates have blamed me for giving away to Miss Dix this valued relic but there are extenuating circumstances. She went to Fortress Monroe to plead in my behalf for justice from my fierce oppressor General Butler... & all because I refused to take the oath of allegiance to the federal government. Then she came to see me, about it, & to comfort me in my trouble, I was very grateful for her kindness, & said I would give her whatever in the house she most wished for, & she chose one of the curtains.*

As the war ended and Reconstruction began, Sallie lived her last few years in the family home in Williamsburg. She survived financial troubles and continued to be a friend to the inmates of the asylum. Although she often admitted that Federal officials had treated her fairly during the occupation, the war had left her with no love at all for the Union. Before she died, she wrote:

> *When I say, our country, I mean the South, for I claim no allegiance to that wicked country, the United States; preferring during the war, the confiscation of all possessions to taking the oath of allegiance.*

Sallie died quietly in her Williamsburg home in 1880 as an unreconstructed Confederate.

# "Yankee" Bowden

L emuel Jackson Bowden was born in Williamsburg the same week that news arrived of General Andrew Jackson's stunning victory over the British at the Battle of New Orleans. That explained his middle name, but few ever understood why he often seemed to take the less popular view where public opinion was concerned.

Young Lemuel attended the College of William & Mary and studied law, opening a practice in Williamsburg in 1838. Despite being a stubborn man, he became fairly successful, serving three terms as a member of the Virginia House of Delegates in the 1840s and helping to rewrite the state constitution in the early 1850s. In 1856, he purchased land adjacent to the church from Bruton Parish, and using his brother as a contractor, erected a fine brick house on the main street.

As the nation began to take sides in 1860, Bowden served as a presidential elector for the Constitutional Union Party, rejecting the radical views of the secessionists. After Lincoln's election, Bowden publicly opposed secession, which immediately made him unpopular with his neighbors. His children, Thomas and Mary, supported his stand, along with his brother Henry, another avowed Unionist. The name "Bowden" became hated in Williamsburg. The sole family member who supported secession was his widowed mother, Mildred, who called her son a traitor to the state and immediately moved out of the fine brick house to take up residence in a small cottage in the rear.

As Virginia joined the Confederacy and active military operations began, Bowden's vocal support of the Union pushed the local authorities to order

Lemuel J. Bowden's house in Williamsburg. *Author's collection.*

his arrest and detention. He was forewarned and quietly slipped out of town, along with his sons, to hide on a family farm in James City County. His brother's family and his daughter, Mary, remained in the family home in town and became the targets of threats.

When the Union army occupied Williamsburg on May 6, 1862, Lemuel Bowden returned to town in triumph. He was on hand to greet McClellan's army as it pursued the retreating Confederates toward Richmond. As the Ninety-Eighth New York Infantry passed through Williamsburg on May 8, the regiment's colonel noted:

> *Before one of the more humble dwellings, sat Lemuel Bowden in a chair; among the faithless, faithful only he. A Union man and a distinguished lawyer....With light hair, red face and gray eyes, he sat, friendly, smiling, bowing to us all as we passed his home.*

The residents of the town did not share the same pleasant opinion of Lemuel J. Bowden. With the Federal occupation, the authorities made him mayor of the town, replacing the elected mayor, Dr. Robert Garrett. It was just one more action in what resident Harriett Cary termed a "Reign of Terror." On May 14, upon hearing a Union army band playing outside of the Bowden House, she noted in her diary:

*The Band serenaded Mayor Bowden tonight—loud cheering heard in conclusion. Down with the Traitor! If we ever recover our power—*

Mayor Bowden immediately set about taking control of the Eastern State Lunatic Asylum and removing all staff who had displayed Confederate sympathies. He placed his brother Henry in charge and gave paid positions to his wife and son. Their "reign," however, did not last long. As McClellan's army was pushed away from Richmond by General Robert E. Lee, the retreating Federals began to pass through the town in August, moving in the opposite direction from the route they had taken three months earlier. As it seemed that Williamsburg was going to be abandoned to the Confederates, Mayor Bowden and his family hastily packed up and left for the safety of Norfolk.

Lemuel J. Bowden's grave in the Congressional Cemetery. *Photograph by Mike Peel (www.mikepeel.net).*

Although the Union army maintained control of the town, Bowden never returned. In 1863, he attended the Wheeling Convention, which claimed to represent the "loyal" State of Virginia and helped form the new state of West Virginia. Bowden was elected to the U.S. Senate but served for less than a year before dying of smallpox on January 2, 1864. He was buried in the Congressional Cemetery.

His son and daughter both remained loyal to the Union. Thomas became the attorney general for both the 1863 restored state of Virginia and later for the Reconstructionist government in Richmond. Mary married a Union soldier from New York whom she had met in Williamsburg during the occupation. Her husband, Charles Porter, served as a representative in the Reconstructionist government of Virginia. Thomas and Mary sold the family house in Williamsburg after the war. Their grandmother Mildred, who had remained loyal to the Confederacy, remained in Williamsburg, dying there in 1874.

# THE RED-LEGGED DEVILS

O ne of the more unusual military units that passed through Williamsburg in 1862 was the Fifth New York Volunteer Infantry. Although they were not greeted with the same hospitality that would mark the Williamsburg area 150 years later, these "visitors" had not arrived for a vacation. Recruited in New York City in April 1861, the unit was mustered into Federal service just ten days after the Confederate firing on Fort Sumter. Colonel Abram Duryee, a wealthy mahogany merchant who had previously commanded an elite New York militia unit, was elected to command the new regiment.

Determined that his new command would also be an elite unit, Duryee selected a colorful uniform patterned after the famous French Zouaves who had met with military success in North Africa and the Crimean War. Outfitted with short blue jackets, baggy red trousers and tasseled fezzes, the Fifth New York came to be known as Duryee's Zouaves. Colonel Duryee spent his first month filling the ranks and vigorously drilling his men. The Fifth New York Volunteer Infantry would be "a glory for the state," he declared.

On May 23, 1861, the regiment paraded down Broadway through cheering crowds and left New York to join the Federal army in the field. The next two years would more than validate Colonel Duryee's opinion of them as a first-rate unit, but it would come at a cost. Of the 848 men who left New York, fewer than 300 of the original volunteers would return home with the regiment.

The regiment was quickly transported to Fort Monroe on the tip of the Virginia's Tidewater Peninsula, where they joined the command of

Colonel Abram Duryee. *Library of Congress.*

General Benjamin Butler. While there, Colonel Duryee began to conduct reconnaissance expeditions in the surrounding Virginia countryside. In the nearby town of Hampton, which had been recently abandoned by its Confederate inhabitants, during a march, one member of the unit inquired of a former slave as to where all the people were. He was told:

> *Dey didn't care for dem yoder sojers, but when dey seen you red-legged debbils comin' right past, dey grab up eberything dey kin and run like the old boy was arter 'em.*

This delighted the New Yorkers, and Private George Tiebout of Company A wrote to his family, "Our regiment is called the red-legged devils, and the terror to evil doers."

Unfortunately, the local Rebels had not run very far, and the regiment received its baptism of fire just a few miles up the Virginia peninsula at Big Bethel on June 10. In a bungled fight, the regiment became part of an attempt to surprise an entrenched Confederate force. The attack failed, and the short battle was called "an inglorious affair." In a hopeless charge, thirty-one of the New Yorkers were killed or wounded, including Private Tiebout.

A group of Duryee's Zouaves at Fort Monroe in 1861. *Library of Congress.*

After the Union defeat at Manassas in July 1861, the regiment was dispatched to guard Washington, D.C., then transferred to Baltimore to help keep maintain order in the pro-Southern city. While there, they were reorganized into General George McClellan's new Army of the Potomac. Colonel Duryee received a promotion to general and left the regiment for staff duty, but the men still proudly referred to themselves as Duryee's Zouaves.

In early 1862, they returned to Virginia as part of General McClellan's grand Peninsula Campaign along with 120,000 Federal troops who landed at Fort Monroe. As they began the march up the peninsula, moving toward the Confederate capital at Richmond, they dug in at Yorktown and took note of the daunting Confederate defensive works. One New Yorker commented that the "big, black guns were as thick as crows in an unprotected cornfield." The next several weeks were spent sharpshooting at the Confederates and making occasional sorties.

Back home in New York, family and friends were kept informed by the numerous correspondents traveling with the army. The *New York Times* reported, "The Fifth Regiment of New York Volunteers is considered the best drilled regiment in the army before Yorktown." General McClellan himself stated that "the Fifth is the best disciplined and soldierly regiment in the Army" and attached the "red-legged devils" to General George Sykes' Division of United States Regulars.

They were not destined to remain at Yorktown long, however. During the night of May 3, 1862, the Confederates abandoned their lines and began a retreat toward Williamsburg. Early the next morning, the soldiers of the Fifth New York found the Rebel earthworks across from them empty. Hardly believing what they discovered, one New Yorker commented, "There was nothing left to fight." McClellan's cavalry quickly located the Confederates, though, and two days later, the Battle of Williamsburg occurred just a few miles away.

Although they were spoiling for a fight, Duryee's Zouaves did not take part in the battle. As the fighting raged around Williamsburg, they were still back at Yorktown waiting to join the march westward. In fact, much of McClellan's army didn't even know that a battle was in progress until it was almost over. They shared in the celebration, though, as news arrived of the capture of Williamsburg. The Fifth observed the occasion with a performance by its band.

Finally, on May 9, the New Yorkers left Yorktown and trudged to Williamsburg. The march was long and hot, causing many of the men to fall, exhausted, by the roadside before they reached the town. Tramping down the road toward Williamsburg, the regiment passed a sloping field that contained several graves of recently buried Confederate dead. Nearby, on a line of ragged and dirty tents, the New Yorkers took note of a message left for them. Ominously written in charcoal on the side of one of the tents were the words "Come along, Yank, there's room outside to bury you."

Upon entering Williamsburg, the regiment marched down the main street, and one soldier noted, "The village of Williamsburg was a beautifully romantic, dreamy old town, the streets being regularly laid out, the houses neat and clean." Some members of the regiment even managed to fit in a little sightseeing.

During the unit's short stay in Williamsburg, one "red-legged devil," Private Charles Baldwin, found a souvenir. Originally from New Jersey, he joined the regiment in Baltimore. Somewhere in town, members of Baldwin's company found a Confederate flag. They cut it up and divided the fragments amongst themselves. Private Baldwin proudly claimed two small pieces and later sent his keepsake back home. In a letter to his mother in Newark, Baldwin wrote:

*I enclose a piece of the rebel flag that was taken in Wmsburg. I have carried it in my pocket ever since take good care of it and don't sell it or give any away.*

Private Baldwin never returned home to tell the whole story of his "rebel flag." He was killed at the Battle of Second Manassas three months after his visit to Williamsburg. His souvenir survived, however, and in 1991, the family returned the two small fragments of flag, along with Baldwin's letter, to the town. Today, these small remembrances of a "red-legged devil's" stay in Williamsburg reside in the collections of the Colonial Williamsburg Foundation.

# A Yankee Sutler

According to the U.S. army regulations of the period, each regiment could have one sutler selected by the commissioned officers of the regiment. A sutler was a civilian entrepreneur who was allowed the privilege of providing foodstuffs and personal items to the soldiers at a profit—very similar to the idea of a modern post exchange. During the Civil War, both sides permitted sutlers to accompany their military units into the field.

In the Northern armies, regimental sutlers were regulated by an act of Congress regarding their business dealings with the troops and were restricted as to what they could sell or charge for their goods. Notwithstanding that, most soldiers found that these "official" merchants charged exorbitant rates for their merchandise, sometimes making profits of several hundred percent. A partial list of accepted sutlery goods included dried apples, oranges, lemons, cheese, raisins, boots, shirt buttons, newspapers, books, tobacco, shoe blacking, toothbrushes, handkerchiefs, stationery and so forth. The sale of alcohol was strictly forbidden.

In 1862, Jacob Aub, a Union army sutler with the Fifth Pennsylvania Cavalry, advertised that he would be conducting business on Williamsburg's main street. With the Federal occupation of the town, he apparently saw an opportunity to make an additional profit from the local population. The officers of the Fifth Pennsylvania must have looked the other way, for the enterprising Aub seems to have imported several items that were never

A typical Union army sutler's tent. *Library of Congress.*

included in army regulations. The following notice appeared in the July 30, 1862 issue of the *Cavalier*, which was printed in Williamsburg by the soldiers of the Fifth Pennsylvania Cavalry:

*FRESH ARRIVAL.*

*WILL BE OPENED ON SATURDAY. August 2nd, a full assortment of goods just arrived from the North, consisting of the following:*

*GROCERIES.*
*Sugar, Tea, Coffee, Salt, Spices, Cheese, Brooms, Buckets, Soap, Candles, Smoked Beef, Prime Sugar, Cured Hams, Sheeps Tongue, &c., &c., &c.*

*DRY GOODS.*
*Calico, Lawn, Berege, Ladies' Dusters, Bleached and Unbleached Cottons,*
*&c., &c., &c.*

*BOOTS AND SHOES.*
*Ladies' Morocco Boots and Slippers, Gentlemen's Gaitors, Children and*
*Misses Boots and Shoes.*

*Sugar, Tobacco, Perfumery, Medicines, &c., &c.*

*Jacob Aub,*
*Sutler, 5th Penn. Cavalry,*
*Main St.*

*Williamsburgh, Va.*

Doubtless, many of Aub's luxuries were in short supply amongst the inhabitants of Williamsburg. With the occupation of the city, local merchants who remained open were hard pressed to obtain goods. Due to the secessionist feelings of the townspeople, especially the women, it is uncertain how successful Aub's business venture was, but it's fairly certain that he didn't sell many pairs of ladies' morocco slippers to the troops of the Fifth Pennsylvania Cavalry.

# COURTSHIP AND A WEDDING

In August 1862, McClellan and his army returned through Williamsburg, going in the opposite direction this time. After taking command of the new Army of Northern Virginia, Confederate general Robert E. Lee had driven McClellan back from the gates of Richmond in the Seven Days Battles of June and July. It was a time of temporary joy for the citizens of the town to see the "hated invaders" returning in defeat.

A Confederate song of the period was titled "Richmond Is a Hard Road to Trabel." It was a parody of a popular minstrel show tune and made fun of the various Union commanders who had tried and failed to take the Confederate capital. One verse spoke of the battle at Williamsburg and how McClellan was foiled by Confederate general James Longstreet and two of his subordinates, Generals Daniel and Ambrose P. Hill:

*Then McClellan followed soon, both with spade and balloon,*
*To try the Peninsular approaches,*
*But one and all agreed that his best rate of speed*
*was no faster than the slowest of "slow coaches."*
*Instead of easy ground, at Williamsburg he found,*
*a Longstreet and indeed nothing shorter.*
*And it put him in the dumps, that his spades wasn't trumps,*
*and the Hills he couldn't level as he ought'er.*

Sallie Galt, now living in her family home on the east end of town, took note of the Federal withdrawal:

> *We have on this peninsula seen War in all its phases, two advancing armies, & two retreating armies almost as large as any the world ever saw. McClellan's army was estimated at one hundred & ninety thousand.... When they retreated we talked to numbers of them, who used to stop under a huge apple tree covered with apples, which grows in our garden.... They would ask for them, & then tell us of the battles between here & Richmond.*

Although the campaign had come to an end, and the Federal army was leaving the peninsula, Williamsburg was not yet to be abandoned by Union troops. As the largest town between Hampton and Richmond, Williamsburg was chosen to be the limit of federal control in that direction. Williamsburg and the area east of town became part of the Department of Virginia under General John Dix, who was headquartered at Fort Monroe. This meant that while the town would remain under the control of a Federal garrison and provost marshal, the area directly to the west of the city was still Confederate.

It was at this time that a rather extraordinary wedding occurred in town that had begun with a courtship born of unusual circumstances. During the battle outside the town on May 5, 1862, a Confederate brigade under General Jubal A. Early made a deadly charge. One of the regiments involved was the Fifth North Carolina Infantry. After entering thick woods a little to the northeast of Williamsburg, the regiment lost contact with the rest of the brigade and emerged just as the Twenty-Fourth Virginia Infantry, led by General Early himself, was advancing toward a brigade of Union troops under General Winfield Scott Hancock to the left.

Hancock's brigade charging the Rebels as pictured in *Harper's Weekly*, May 1862. *National Archives.*

*Left*: Major General Winfield Scott Hancock. *Library of Congress.*

*Right*: Captain John Willis Lea, Fifth North Carolina Infantry. *Colonial Williamsburg Foundation (used with permission from Mrs. J.W. Lea Jr.).*

The North Carolinians wheeled in support of the Virginians and found themselves under a murderous fire. The North Carolinian commander, Lieutenant Colonel John C. Badham, attempted to encourage his men by shouting, "Now we've got the damned Yankees, give them Bull Run and Ball's Bluff." His men charged forward, joining the Virginians in shouting, "Bull Run! Bull Run!" Colonel Badham went down, shot through the forehead. In just a few minutes of battle, the Fifth North Carolina had 302 men, killed, wounded or missing; the Virginians also had about 200 casualties.

Left behind among the wounded North Carolinians on that muddy field was twenty-three-year-old John Willis Lea. Originally from South Carolina, Lea had resided in Caswell County, North Carolina, before the war. He attended the U.S. Military Academy at West Point but had resigned at the beginning of the war and "gone south." There, he was commissioned as the captain of Company I, Fifth North Carolina Infantry, in May 1861. One year later, as he lay in a barn that was being used as a field hospital near Williamsburg, a former West Point classmate, Lieutenant George Armstrong Custer, recognized Captain Lea.

George Custer had been out of West Point less than a year, having graduated early to help meet the urgent need for officers. Though he graduated at the bottom of his class, he was at the beginning of a career that would eventually lead him to the Little Bighorn River in Montana in 1876. Custer had been present at the First Battle of Manassas and was now on detached duty from the Fifth U.S. Cavalry, serving on the staff of General William F. "Baldy" Smith. In that capacity, he had already distinguished himself by ascending several times in a military balloon at Yorktown and gathering information about the Confederate withdrawal.

At Williamsburg, he had verified valuable intelligence provided by a contraband slave regarding a way around the Confederate lines. He personally scouted the route and then led General Winfield Scott Hancock's brigade into position on the same field where Early's brigade would attack. During the subsequent fighting, Custer claimed he captured the first Confederate battle flag of the campaign—the flag of the Fifth North

Lieutenant George Armstrong Custer in camp two weeks after the Battle of Williamsburg. *Library of Congress.*

Carolina Infantry. The apparent truth, however, is that it was captured by an enlisted man and given to Custer.

In the hospital barn on the field at Williamsburg, Custer and his former classmate Lea greeted each other so warmly that onlookers believed them to be brothers. Lieutenant Custer gave Lea a pair of stockings and some money. Lea reciprocated by writing a request in Custer's notebook:

*Wmsburg, 5-6-62—If ever Lt. Custer, U.S.A., should be taken prisoner, I want him treated as well as he has treated me. —J. W. Lea, Capt., C.S.A.*

Later that night, Custer returned to his duties and joined the advance of the Union troops toward Richmond.

During the fighting around Richmond, Custer was promoted to captain and appointed to the staff of General McClellan. Curiously, he would soon find another West Point classmate who had become a Confederate officer. On May 31, at the Battle of Seven Pines, Lieutenant James B. Washington of Maryland, the great-grandnephew of George Washington, was captured as he stumbled into Union lines. Upon recognizing him, Custer took the opportunity to visit and even had a nearby photographer take several images of them together.

Meanwhile, back in Williamsburg, romance blossomed. Lea and another wounded Southerner, a Lieutenant Hays, were taken into the home of Colonel Goodrich Durfey. Living in Colonel Durfey's household was his young daughter, Margaret, who was just seventeen years old. Margaret personally took over the care of Captain Lea. Within a short time, the two began to take an interest in one another. The diary entry of another young lady, Harriette Cary, permits a glance at this budding love just two weeks after the battle:

*Spent the rest of the day at Col. D's where there are two of our wounded— very interesting gentlemen, Capt. Lea and Lieutenant Hays, both doing quite well—the former the happiest soul I ever saw.*

By the end of the month, Captain Lea had recovered enough to be able to get around on crutches. Within the next two months, after obtaining the permission of her father, he and Margaret announced their engagement.

It is through the eyes of Custer that we observe the rest of the story. After the Seven Days Battles around Richmond, and as the Federal army

*Right*: Margaret Durfey. *Colonial Williamsburg Foundation (used with permission from Mrs. J.W. Lea Jr.).*

*Below*: The Durfey House, where Captain John Willis Lea wed Margaret Durfey, is now known as Bassett Hall. *Special Collections, John D. Rockefeller Jr. Library, Colonial Williamsburg Foundation.*

returned to Fort Monroe in August 1862, Captain Custer passed through Williamsburg once more. There, he discovered that his classmate was still in town recuperating from his wound. After asking for directions, he made his way to the Durfey house. Upon his arrival and amid their reunion, it was decided that the nuptials should proceed immediately, and Custer should be the best man.

Custer wrote to his sister that he was present at the Durfey house long before the appointed hour. He told how both the bride and her bridesmaid, Margaret's cousin Maggie, were dressed in white with a wreath of flowers adorning each girl's head:

> *I never saw two prettier girls. Lea was dressed in a bright new rebel uniform trimmed with gold lace; I wore my full uniform of blue. The minister arrived, and at nine we took our places upon the floor. L. made the responses in a clear and distinct tone. The bride made no response whatever except to the first question; she was evidently confused, though she afterwards said (laughing) that she neglected to respond purposely so as to be free from any obligations.*

Custer went on further in his letter, telling of a joke Captain Lea pulled on Maggie:

> *Everyone seemed happy except the young lady who had been my partner on the floor. She kissed the bride and sat down crying. Lea, observing this, said, "Why Cousin Maggie, what are you crying for? There is nothing to cry about. Oh, I know. You are crying because you are not married; well, here is the minister and here is Captain Custer, who I know would be glad to carry off such a pretty bride from the Confederacy." She managed to reply, "Captain Lea, you are just as mean as you can be."*

After obtaining an official leave of absence from his military duties, Custer remained with the wedding party at Colonel Durfey's house for two weeks. He concluded the letter to his sister by writing:

> *Cousin Maggie would regale me by singing and playing on the piano, "My Maryland," "Dixie", "For Southern Rights, Hurrah," etc. We were all fond of cards and would play for the Southern Confederacy. When doing so Lea and I were the only players, while the ladies were spectators. He won, every time, when playing for the Confederacy, he representing the South, I*

*the North. Lea has since been exchanged and is now fighting for what he supposes are his rights.*

Although Margaret Durfey enjoyed a lovely wedding and honeymoon, it was marred by the fact that her new husband, Captain Lea, was a prisoner of war. When he finally recuperated from his Williamsburg wound, he was sent to Fort Monroe and then north under confinement. Upon his exchange as a prisoner, Captain Lea rejoined the Fifth North Carolina Infantry. He was wounded again at Chancellorsville in 1863 and again a third time at Winchester in September 1864.

Lea ended the war as a colonel, commanding a brigade, and met his former West Point classmate, now Major General Custer, one last time at Appomattox. The night of the surrender of General Lee, on April 9, 1865, the two old classmates shared dinner in Custer's tent and talked of old times. In the following days, the newly paroled Colonel Lea returned to Williamsburg and Margaret to begin their life together and raise a family. He later became an Episcopal priest, and they moved to a new home in West Virginia, where he served several parishes.

# WILLIAMSBURG AND THE LITTLE BIGHORN

When Captain George Armstrong Custer passed through Williamsburg and served as the best man in a local wedding, no one could have guessed that he would later achieve fame as a cavalry commander against the Indian tribes on the western plains. Although he ended the war as a major general, he was reduced to the rank of lieutenant colonel in the much smaller postwar army.

Assigned as the second-in-command of the newly formed Seventh U.S. Cavalry, he embarked on a new phase of his military career that would take him far from the old city of Williamsburg. His career eventually ended in 1876 in Montana at the Battle of the Little Bighorn, where he and 268 men under his command died. Custer, however, was not the only ill-fated member of the Seventh Cavalry to serve in and around Williamsburg during the Civil War.

On May 4, 1862, Federal cavalry under General Stoneman began a pursuit of the retreating Confederates who had just abandoned their lines at Yorktown and were passing through Williamsburg. While approaching the city, the Union horsemen became engaged with Confederate cavalry (under General J.E.B. Stuart) who were acting as a rearguard. In a prelude to the Battle of Williamsburg, a skirmish developed. As the rebels overran a Federal cannon that was stuck in the mud, elements of the First U.S. Cavalry charged forward to save the gun.

Among the charging horsemen that day was a young captain named Marcus A. Reno. Reno had barely managed to obtain a commission, as he graduated from the U.S. Military Academy two years late, in 1857, because of excessive demerits. Assigned to the First Cavalry in 1861, he was commanding Troop H on the field at Williamsburg. As Reno and his men surged forward, they recaptured the lost gun along with several Confederate prisoners. The First Cavalry then took up a defensive position and awaited the arrival of Federal infantry.

Although Reno and his men would not be seriously involved in the Battle of Williamsburg the next day, Reno was among the first to enter the city on May 6. They remained almost a week, and

A postwar photograph of Major Marcus Reno. *Wikimedia Commons, Denver Library Digital Collection.*

Reno surely had time to look around the old colonial capital. Captain Reno would go on to have an impressive war record; he was cited for bravery and brevetted to higher rank several times. He ended the war as a brevet brigadier general of U.S. Volunteers.

With the postwar reduction, he received the rank of major and was appointed to the Seventh U.S. Cavalry in 1869. Although he was not a favorite of the regiment's acting commander, Lieutenant Colonel Custer, Reno found himself serving as second-in-command during the fighting at the Little Bighorn on June 25, 1876. His battalion held out on a hill that day and survived. His later life would always be colored by his actions during that battle. Even though a court of inquiry cleared him of charges against his conduct at the Little Bighorn, he was court-martialed twice for conduct unbecoming to a gentleman. Major Reno was finally dismissed from the army in 1880 and died destitute in Washington, D.C., in 1889.

One other participant in the fighting at Williamsburg was Private Thomas Murray, an Irishman from County Monaghan. After answering the call for volunteers in the days following the attack on Fort Sumter in 1861, Murray enlisted in Company K of the Thirty-Seventh New York Infantry. At Williamsburg, he took part in General Kearny's advance to support General Hooker and the Union's right flank. In a driving rain, Private Murray was severely wounded in his left hand and taken to a dressing station on the field. After heading to New York City to recuperate, he was promoted to sergeant and mustered out on July 22, 1862.

Murray's wound at Williamsburg did not dampen his spirit, for he reenlisted two days later in Battery I of the Thirteenth New York Heavy Artillery. His battery was attached to the Naval Brigade of the Army of the James, guarding shipping on the James River during the Siege of Petersburg. He finished the war and was mustered out a second time in August 1865.

Apparently disenchanted with civilian life and peacetime, Murray reenlisted once again on August 17, 1866. Having previously served in the infantry and artillery, he now chose the cavalry, entering Troop B of the Seventh Cavalry. He was promoted to sergeant a second time in 1871.

In 1876, Murray accompanied Lieutenant Colonel Custer to the Little Big Horn. On June 25, he was part of the supply pack train when he entered the fighting at Major Reno's beleaguered position on the bluffs overlooking the Little Bighorn River. Fiercely attacked and under heavy fire, Sergeant Murray directed the pack train and brought Reno's men needed ammunition and supplies. That night and the following day, the troopers on Reno Hill fought off attacking enemies and the heat and thirst. During that time, although he was wounded, Murray continued to move conspicuously, distributing ammunition and rations.

Reno and his command were unaware of Custer's fate until they were relieved by General Alfred Terry's relief column on June 28. Afterward, nineteen men were awarded the Medal of Honor for distinguishing themselves during their ordeal. Among them was Sergeant Thomas Murray. The citation for his award stated:

> *The President of the United States of America, in the name of Congress, takes pleasure in presenting the Medal of Honor to Sergeant Thomas Murray, United States Army, for extraordinary heroism on 25 June 1876, while serving with Company B, 7th U.S. Cavalry, in action at Little Big Horn, Montana. Sergeant Murray brought up the pack train, and on the second day the rations, under a heavy fire from the enemy.*

Although it was several years and many miles away from the fighting at Williamsburg in 1862, fate had brought George Custer, Marcus Reno and Thomas Murray together at the Little Bighorn for one more desperate battle.

# EMANCIPATION

On the eve of the Civil War, about half of Williamsburg's population was African American. The 1860 census enumerated 748 slaves and 121 free blacks or mulattos, with another 19 of undetermined status listed at the Eastern State Lunatic Asylum.

In Tidewater Virginia as a whole, the tobacco economy of the eighteenth and early nineteenth centuries had moved farther west in the state, and food production became a primary agricultural pursuit. Slaves worked former tobacco land that now contained large crops of wheat, corn, potatoes, peas, oats and various fruits in abundance. Additionally, many slaves and freemen worked as watermen, fishing and gathering oysters in the James and York Rivers and the Chesapeake Bay.

The great majority of slaves within the city proper, however, were not agricultural field slaves but rather house servants and various specialty tradesmen. They usually resided either in or near the homes of their Williamsburg masters. Some were rented out to serve other masters in town.

When the war began, local military authorities commenced construction of defensive works outside of town to obstruct any Union advance toward Richmond. To provide manpower for this purpose, authorities hired free black laborers and conscripted slaves both male and female. The Confederate government paid free blacks fifty cents per day for unskilled laborers and one dollar per day for skilled carpenters or bricklayers. Masters whose slaves were conscripted were paid at the same rate for their use.

Slaves in Williamsburg were also called upon to serve in other ways. They refitted buildings to serve as hospitals, tended to the influx of sick soldiers and accompanied the army as military cooks. The arrival of refugees and soldiers to the city also doubtless provided new income to the town's black seamstresses and washerwomen.

The close presence of Federal troops on Virginia's Lower Peninsula presented slaves with an enticing chance at freedom. Throughout 1861, area slaves began running to Hampton and nearby Fort Monroe. At the same time, however, runaway slaves presented Federal commanders with a thorny problem. Slavery was still legal under federal law, and the Fugitive Slave Law of 1850 required Federal authorities to assist in the return of runaway slaves to their masters.

Union general Benjamin Butler, commanding at Fort Monroe, was directly confronted with the problem just after Virginia left the Union and joined the Confederacy. Three runaway slaves arrived at his headquarters at Fort Monroe and asked for refuge, claiming that they were going to be sent south by their master to work on Confederate fortifications. At the same time, their master, now a Confederate officer, requested that Butler return his "property" as required by the Fugitive Slave Law.

Butler, who worked as a lawyer before the war, devised a solution; since the Virginians proclaimed they had left the Union, then the law did not apply to them. Furthermore, because the Confederates considered the slaves to be property, Butler declared that under international law, he was justified in confiscating that property if it was being used to wage war against the United States. To Butler, the slaves became "contraband of war." He agreed to return the slaves, however, if their owner would personally come to his headquarters and take an oath of allegiance to the United States. The slaves were not reclaimed, and this set a precedent. As word spread among the African American population on the Virginia Peninsula, there was a rapid increase in runaway slaves traveling to Fort Monroe. The term "contraband" was soon applied to refugee slaves who were seeking protection and freedom. Contraband camps sprang up around Hampton and Fort Monroe and were protected by Federal troops.

With the battle outside Williamsburg in May 1862 and the establishment of Federal authority in the city, most of the remaining slaves in town quickly left their masters, but a number stayed—mostly the elderly—due to loyalty to various families. Many of the free blacks and mulattos stayed simply because Williamsburg was their home. Several blacks felt that Williamsburg was so much their home that they served the Confederacy even after Federal

Contraband slaves near Williamsburg, 1862. *Library of Congress.*

occupation. One free black washerwoman and cook, Roctilda Rollerson, worked for the Federal provost marshal of Williamsburg while simultaneously passing on military information to the Confederates outside the town.

Many slaves seized the opportunity to be of assistance in the fight against their former masters. During the Battle of Williamsburg on May 5, 1862, at least sixteen local slaves made their way to the Union commanders on the field, offering information about the Confederates and their defenses.

Besides the government-sanctioned contraband camps established near the city, some slaves hid in unofficial colonies of refugees, and a few ex-slaves began to commit crimes in the local countryside. In October 1862, the citizens of Williamsburg were horrified to learn of the murder of three whites by runaway slaves on nearby Jamestown Island. With the ever-present Southern fear of slave rebellion in mind, at least one Williamsburg resident, Mrs. M.N. Munford, wrote to Union general Henry M. Naglee complaining about the local depredations.

The new year of 1863 brought with it the Emancipation Proclamation. Although area slaves had been protected as contraband, that was not true freedom. Theoretically, if the South won the war, the contraband slaves might have had to be returned. Also, the property rights of slave owners of Williamsburg were protected under the Fugitive Slave Law, which was still in effect. Even though the Federal army occupied the city, slaves who remained with their masters and did not run were still slaves. This changed with the Emancipation Proclamation.

Susie Melton, a slave living near Williamsburg, later remembered "that night of freedom":

> *I was a young gal 'bout ten years ole, an' we done heard dat Lincum gonna turn de niggers free. Ole missus says dey warn't nothin' to it. Den a Yankee soldier tole someone in Williamsburg dat Marse Lincum done signed de 'Mancipation. Was winter time an moughty cold dat night, but ev'ybody commence gittin' ready to leave. Didn't care nothin' 'bout Missus—was goin' to de Union lines. An' all dat night de niggers danced an' sang right out in de cold. Nex' mornin' at daybreak we all started out wid blankets an' clothes an' pots an' pans an' chickens piled on our backs, 'cause Missus said we couldn't take no horses or carts. An' as de sun come up over de trees de niggers all started to singin':*

> *Sun, you be here and I'll be gone*
> *Sun, you be here and I'll be gone*
> *Sun, you be here and I'll be gone*
> *Bye, bye, don't grieve after me*
> *Won't give you my place, not for yours*
> *Bye, bye, don't grieve after me*
> *Cause you be here and I'll be gone*

At the moment it was issued (January 1, 1863), the Emancipation Proclamation could not be enforced in areas still in rebellion. In the South as a whole, between twenty-five thousand and seventy-five thousand slaves who lived in areas where Federal troops were active were immediately emancipated. However, the proclamation specifically exempted the forty-eight counties that formed the new state of West Virginia, which were not considered secessionist territory. Also excluded were the Virginia counties of Accomack, Northampton, Elizabeth City, York, Princess Anne and Norfolk. (See Appendix E.)

These counties were deemed to be under Federal occupation. The remaining area of Virginia was under Confederate control and covered under the terms of the proclamation, but for practical purposes, Federal mandates could not be enforced until Federal troops occupied a specific locale.

Williamsburg itself fell under a difficult interpretation of the proclamation. Under the wording of the proclamation, only slaves in areas still in rebellion against the United States government were to be considered free. The city of Williamsburg was occupied and under martial law within Federal control. Geographically, however, the northern half of the city was in York County, which was specifically mentioned as an exempted county, and the southern half was in James City County, which was still considered to be under Confederate control and was covered under the proclamation. The dividing line between the two counties was the main street of the town, the Duke of Gloucester Street, that ran from east to west. This led to the question of the validity of the proclamation within the city limits. Who was free, and who was a slave? The Federal provost marshal seems to have taken matters into his own hands. Eliza Baker remembered:

> *The Provost Marshal lived in Mr. Saunders' House on the Palace Green. His name was Wheeling. I went up there one day to ask him could I go out to see my mother in the country and would he give me a pass for the next Sunday. He said, "What you want to wait till Sunday for?" And I said, "Cause I can't go till Sunday. I have to work for Mrs. Whiting." And he said, "You can go when you want to. You are just as free as she is!" He gave me a pass for Tuesday. So I went back to the house. The children told their mother about my askin' for the pass and about what the Marshal had said to me. I went upstairs and got my dress (I only had two), and that night I took out and went down home, and I ain't never been back to the Whitings since!*

One way or the other, the Emancipation Proclamation changed life for Williamsburg's African American population regardless of whether they were free or slaves.

# A Confederate Raid

After August 1862, occupied Williamsburg sat on the edge of Federal control and authority. Southern cavalry and partisans soon began operating in the area west of town, constantly observing the Federal lines and harassing Union troops whenever the opportunity presented itself.

At dawn on the morning of September 9, 1862, Confederate raiders galloped into the city, capturing the picket guards at the west end of town, and made a prisoner of the acting provost marshal, Colonel David Campbell of the Fifth Pennsylvania Cavalry. Williamsburg was again in Confederate hands, and the inhabitants came out into the streets to give news and provisions to the raiders. Writing after the war, one woman recalled:

> Such a scene of the wildest tumult and joy can only be imagined by those who have felt the sudden uplifting of the oppressors heel. Women laughed and wept, wrung the hands of strangers, imploring Heavens blessing upon them and the Cause for which they fought; In the wild delirium of the moment no thought came of the rude aftermath that would follow upon the retreat of the Confederates.

The town's joy did not last long. Federal reinforcements from east of town soon had the Confederate raiders retreating, and after a few hours of freedom, the city was again occupied. That afternoon, several troopers of the Fifth Pennsylvania Cavalry, having gotten drunk, apparently started a fire that consumed the main building of the College of William & Mary. In a deposition taken later, Mary T. Southall stated

Troopers of the Fifth Pennsylvania Cavalry. *Library of Congress.*

*that she resided at the time on the College grounds at the President's house, and that she was alarmed on the evening of the 8th of September by the cry of fire. She went out and found that the College building was on fire, that soon a crowd gathered and extinguished the flames; and that while carrying a bucket of water she met three United States soldiers; one of them told her if the College was not burned that day it would be the next, or words to that effect; that early the next day a detachment of the Southern Cavalry entered and after a short contest retired, the last one leaving by ten minutes after ten o'clock A.M.; that shortly afterward the college yard was crowded with United States soldiers, many of them drunk and boisterous; that she and her sisters were advised, so unruly were they, to leave the premises, which they did; that about five o'clock P.M. she was told of the College being on fire and advised to return as the house in which she lived was in great danger. This she did, and soon after the college was a smoking ruin; and that there is no doubt of the destruction having been designedly effected by drunken United States soldiers.*

Besides setting the college on fire, some of the Federals took out their anger on nearby citizens. Mrs. C.B.T. Coleman wrote of an incident about which she had been told:

*Some of the citizens had made themselves peculiarly obnoxious to the Yankees, and on these their wrath was visited. Mr. C.W., though sick in bed, when he heard the Confederate Cavalry dashing through the street and the clash of sabers managed to reach a window and there with the boots he was unable to draw on, he beat a tattoo of welcome on the Dutch roof of his house, calling out "kill 'em kill 'em." His voice though feeble reached the ears of the Yankees. Bitterly was he made to rue the day, for as soon as it was safe for them to do so the Yankees swarmed into his house, broke up his furniture and destroyed everything they could lay their hands on. Mrs. W. endeavored to prevent their going upstairs to the sick room of her husband and was herself forced to jump with her infant in her arms over the banisters and flee she knew not whither. At this juncture an Officer arrived on the scene and commanded the soldiers to depart, unfortunately, he could not restore order in the dismantled wrecked house.*

Once more, fighting had come to Williamsburg, this time in the very streets of the old colonial capital. Unfortunately, it would happen several more times before the war was through.

# MRS. ANDERSON'S WINE

Always on the lookout for contraband war material and suspecting several townspeople of communicating with Confederate scouts outside the city, the Federal authorities occasionally conducted searches of Williamsburg homes. One resident, Sallie Galt, remembered the invasion of her house:

> We had a whole company of Infantry, from New York City, to search the house for rebels, arms & contraband goods....I think the Capt must have been one of the New York detectives he conducted the search in such a thorough & scientific manner. One of our keys was tyed with a blue ribbon, & a federal soldier said, "I did not think your soldiers would let you have anything blue."

Even though Sallie Galt emerged unscathed from the Federal search, others were not as fortunate. Helen Anderson seemed to have difficulties with the Federal authorities. Anderson was seventy-nine years old when the war came to Williamsburg, and as Union troops entered the city on May 6, 1862, she, like many others, requested protection from the "enemy" for her property. She addressed her request to the Federal commander himself:

*Maj. Gen. Geo. W. [sic] McClellan*
*in Command of U.S. Army Present*

*Illustrious Sir*
    *Being an aged Female of this city, I take the liberty of soliciting your Protection for myself, Household and property under the present truly distressing circumstances. your benevolent attention to this urgent request of mine will be gratefully acknowledged and remembered by me.*
*very respectfully*

*Helen Maxwell Anderson*
*City of Williamsburg*
*May the 6. 1862--*

Helen Anderson received the protection of the provost marshal that same day. First, however, her house was searched for possible contraband. As nothing was found that could be dangerous to the occupying army, a "safeguard" issued to her stated that "no soldier search this house while our troops occupy this place." Helen Anderson appears to not have been bothered further by the Federal authorities until September, when she wrote to Major General John Dix:

*Williamsburg Virginia Sept 13, 1862*
*Maj Genl Dix*

*Sir*
    *My House was broken open this morning by an armed band of soldiers and a large quantity of my valuable old wine, which has been in my family for many years, taken away. This is a heavy loss to me, and one that is irreffarable and I appeal to you to exercise your authority and have it restored to me. Your immediate action is requested, otherwise it will be too late.*
*very respectfully yours*

*please telegraph your order. Your soldiers were led in person by Lieut. Simpson, nephew to Col. Campbell, who is Provost Marshal in Williamsburg now. The excuse made was that they were removed for Confederate Soldiers, but I can assure you that such is not the case.*

*Yours etc.*
*H.M. Anderson*

This plea produced a reply from the provost marshal's office, which tried to placate Helen Anderson. A new guard was offered to prevent her "from being molested," but the wine was taken elsewhere:

*Sept. 13, 1862*

*Mrs. Anderson*
*    The liquor taken from your house this morning by the Provost Marshal to prevent the soldiers from getting it is returned to you, but it must be kept at the Insane Asylum for safe keeping. You can get it there, as you want it—*

*Yours etc.*
*Lt. E. Shultz P.M.A.*
*Comd. Post*

Helen Anderson's wine was stored at the Eastern State Lunatic Asylum and put under the lock and key of Corporal H.M. Flanagan.

Not trusting the good faith of the provost marshal, Anderson once again attempted to write General Dix, through Captain T. Hennessey, asking for his intervention. She added, "a large portion had been consumed by soldiers and negroes." In October, she again wrote Captain Hennessey asking if she was still the owner of the wines.

Unfortunately, Anderson's correspondence ends there, but another related document survives. An inventory taken by Corporal Flanagan reveals that between September 20 and October 1, 1862, he issued out thirty-three bottles of wine on fourteen separate requisitions to several different Federal officers. Only history knows if Helen Anderson ever recovered any of her "valuable old wine."

# THE OATH OF ALLEGIANCE

O n at least three separate occasions during the Federal occupation, the military authorities attempted to force the unrepentant rebel inhabitants of Williamsburg to swear an oath of allegiance to the U.S. government. The first occurred in early 1863.

In the dark, early hours of March 29, 1863, Confederate troops made an unsuccessful attempt to capture Fort Magruder east of town. The attack was possibly staged in retaliation for the closure of Bruton Parish Church that February by the Federal provost marshal after the rector, Reverend Thomas M. Ambler, refused to pray for the president of the United States. As dawn broke, the attack was aborted, and Confederate infantry entered the town from the east, trying to get down the main thoroughfare, Duke of Gloucester Street, and out of town to the west as quickly as possible. Unfortunately, Union cavalry attempted to stop them, which resulted in a skirmish on the main street.

Captain Gustavus A. Wallace of the Fifty-Ninth Virginia Infantry detailed the action:

> *I immediately formed line of battle and advanced at double quick speed and in good order. They seeming to advance, I halted and fired several rounds. Having dispersed them, I marched by flank to the town. Another large body of cavalry in the mean time was discovered in a field on our left, who followed us to the town. When I struck the main street, up which I filed my force, this last body followed. In the mean time we captured 4*

*prisoners, horses, arms, &c., and fired on several who would not surrender. I then discovered about 30 or 40 cavalry forming ahead of us at College Place. Having thus the enemy to contend with at each end of the street I formed my men on the right side of Main street, when the body at College Place advanced in a charge. We held our fire until they were close to us. Our fire broke and confused them. We killed 3 men at this fire and wounded several...I continued to move but made another stand at College place... We did not lose a man.*

As the Confederates withdrew, leaving a haze of gun smoke over the bodies of the Federal cavalrymen lying in the street, the town was reoccupied.

At the time of the raid, Brigadier General Richard Busteed was in temporary command of the Federal troops in Williamsburg. Busteed was described as a "New York lawyer and local politician" who, "never having had military experience of any kind," was embarrassed by the Confederate attack and saw the people of Williamsburg as conspirators in the affair. Only three days before, he had telegraphed the commander of the Department of Virginia, Major General John A. Dix, at Fort Monroe:

*Yorktown, March 26, 1863*
*Major-General DIX*
   *GENERAL: A telegram has just reached me that our pickets at Williamsburg were fired on this morning by a number of the enemy's infantry. A continual warfare of this character is kept up against us at and about the town. I am of the deliberate judgment that the only way of our immunity lies in the destruction of Williamsburg, and if you will approve it I would give the inhabitants notice that upon a repetition of these attacks the place should be destroyed. The town is a stronghold of rank traitors.*
   *RICHARD BUSTEED,*
   *Brigadier-General, Commanding.*

Following the Confederate attack on March 29, he submitted his official report, which stated:

*Our casualties were 5 wounded, 6 missing, and 2 murdered. The boots were stolen from off our dead. The enemy's loss...is at least 18. He came with a train of wagons and four field pieces and was guided into the town by citizens of Williamsburg at three different points.*

Brigadier General Richard Busteed.
*Wikimedia Commons.*

General Busteed was convinced that the "rank traitors" in Williamsburg were the cause of his problems. In answer to the perceived actions of the town's inhabitants, he issued the following general order that would greatly affect the people of Williamsburg:

*The attack of the enemy on our lines at Williamsburg this Sabbath morning was accomplished by circumstances of so aggravated a character as to call for prompt and severe punishment to those most implicated. Conclusive evidence has been furnished to the commanding general that the attack was aided, if not planned, by citizens of Williamsburg, and carried to a successful end by them and their abettors outside the lines; that the enemy were led into the city by one or more citizens, and that when once in they were enabled by the aid of the citizens and their own overwhelming force to occupy the most advantageous points for attack and defense; that upon their occupation of the city they were assisted by the citizens in their attack upon our forces, who were fired upon from the houses lining the streets, the dead bodies of the murdered being despoiled and stripped, their boots pulled off their feet; that the stores of their sympathizers within the city were thrown open to their advantage and their horses loaded with packs prepared for their arrival. To provide against a repetition of the outrage the commanding General directs:*

*1st, -That all the privileges to all storekeepers in the city of Williamsburg to purchase and sell goods are revoked.*

*2nd, -That all citizens in the city of Williamsburg and vicinity who are willing to take the oath of allegiance to the Government of the United States will present themselves to the provost marshal of Williamsburg for the purpose of taking such oath on or before the 1st day of April, 1863.*

*3rd, -That all citizens in the city of Williamsburg and vicinity who are not willing to take the oath of allegiance to the Government of the United States, excepting the servants and employees of the Eastern Lunatic Asylum of the State of Virginia, will prepare themselves and their families to be placed beyond the lines now occupied by the armed forces of the said Govt. by the 2nd day of April, 1863.*

The town's white inhabitants, most of whom were women and children, viewed the order with horror. While their husbands, fathers and sons were away fighting for the Confederacy, most of Williamsburg's residents had no intention of swearing an oath of allegiance to the United States, although at least one woman of the town announced, "I'll sign anything which will make life easier for my people." Others could not bring themselves to take the accursed oath. After the war, Cynthia B.T. Coleman wrote a secondhand account of the experience of Emily Morrison, which reflects the Victorian sentimentality of the time:

*The order was issued for the inhabitants to take the oath of allegiance to the U.S. Government or to abandon their homes....Among those whose narrow means bound them to the spot was Miss Emily Morrison—a name ever to be held in reverence and honour. With an aged and ill mother there was no alternative; stay she must. When the officer arrived to put the test she was in an agony of distress. In vain was the pen placed in her trembling fingers; they had no power to hold it. Her mother from her seemingly dying bed exhorted her not to perjure herself. "Let me not die, my daughter, seeing you take this lie upon your heart. Let me go into the presence of my Maker believing you true to yourself and to your Country." The officer was melted by this scene and left these two noble women in peace.*

The idea of families being thrown out of Williamsburg without any proof of their complicity in the Confederate attack was too much for the higher Federal authorities. The department commander, Major General Dix, countermanded the order of General Busteed within twenty-four hours. In its place, he issued his own directive regarding Williamsburg:

*In view of the raid on Williamsburg on Sunday last, and rumors of complicity on the part of the inhabitants with the assailants, you will give orders as follows:*

*1st-No persons will be allowed to go to Williamsburg from any point south of Fort Magruder without taking the oath of allegiance.*

*2nd-No citizen of Williamsburg will be permitted to go to Yorktown or to any place south of Fort Magruder without taking the oath of allegiance.*

*3rd-No person will be allowed to trade in Williamsburg without first taking the oath of allegiance.*

*4th-No further supplies will be allowed to be taken to Williamsburg for the use of the inhabitants, except the produce of the neighboring farms, until further orders.*

*An investigation will be made into the circumstances alleged to have occurred at the time of the attack, and if the parties accused of aiding and abetting it are detected and reasonable presumption of their guilt is shown they will be brought before a military tribunal and punished according to the laws of war.*

General Dix's order further stated that any house that was found to be used by the Confederates, with the consent of the owner, for the purpose of firing upon U.S. soldiers would be razed to the ground.

Although they were not required to take an oath or else be deported from the town, the people of Williamsburg now found their town sealed off as an island between the Union and Confederacy.

General Busteed, possibly because of his harsh order, found himself relieved of command. Within a week, he resigned from the service. He was subsequently appointed as a U.S. district judge for Alabama, which meant very little at the time, since most of Alabama was under Confederate control. He formally took his seat after the war ended but resigned in 1874 to avoid impeachment.

# THE WAR CONTINUES

J ust as the people of Williamsburg settled down after the latest round of nearby skirmishing, Confederate forces attempted another attack on Union defenses east of the city. The Southerners, under former Virginia governor Henry Wise, now a Confederate general, had been ordered by the Confederate high command in Richmond to try to provoke a battle with the Union troops in the Williamsburg area. It was hoped that a threat toward Williamsburg would draw Union troops away from the defense of Suffolk, Virginia, which was then besieged by Confederate general James Longstreet across the James River fifty miles to the south.

Fighting erupted around the town early on the morning of April 11, 1863. Lieutenant Luther R. Mills of the Twenty-Sixth Virginia Infantry wrote of the attack:

> We entered Williamsburg about sunrise of the eleventh. Our raid was made for the purpose of drawing the enemy's attention from Suffolk, collecting forage and allowing the inhabitants of the town a chance to get away....I will leave you to draw the results of it from the newspapers as I do not wish to destroy the effects of that glorious report by telling you the truth. I will, however, tell you something about the manner in which the affair was managed. Gen. Wise carried us down Main Street in solid column (infantry on both sidewalks and artillery in double column in the center) without clearing the town with skirmishers. Four pieces of artillery at the lower end of town would have destroyed half of the Brigade.

Fortunately for the Confederates, they met with little resistance in Williamsburg proper. The Federals retreated to their fortifications at Fort Magruder and shelled the town. In a letter to his mother, Williamsburg resident John Coupland described the fighting and his efforts to protect his wife and family. His letter offers a glimpse of the hazards faced by civilians in the city:

*Our forces entered the college end of the town & took position at the lower end lining the street from Ma's down to Woodpecker* [York Street]. *The Yankees opened fire from the Fort below and for some time vigorously shelled the town. It was very early in the morning, no one being up in the house but myself when it commenced, and in great hurry and confusion did we put on a few clothes and thrust a few more as change for us into a bag. George and I went to the stable to get the cart & horse and I sent Sue & the children up to Ma's to await us. While hitching the horse a shell burst directly over our heads, but doing no damage; two fell in the garden and 3 within a few feet of the house under our chamber window. One burst in front of the door in the street killing a horse & wounding two men.*

Continuing, Coupland described the extent of the Federal bombardment:

*Mrs. Morrison's kitchen was penetrated by a ball, her porch steps torn up by a shell. She and Miss Emily were in the house. Many other houses were struck and portions of them torn to pieces, but strange to say none took fire. All that portion of the town from the Episcopal Church down embracing much the larger part was pretty well peppered. I took all hands up to the Asylum for protection. I feared the excitement would prove injurious to Sue but she stood it like a hero. Our men withdrew beyond the College and the firing ceased.*

Sallie Galt, still despondent over the death of her brother the year before, also wrote of the Confederate attacks and subsequent Federal reaction:

*We have been shelled twice in eleven days. They are not skirmishing in the streets today, the enemy are just at the end of Woodpecker (York) Street, & came in town this morning 250 of Infantry but <u>seeing</u> our <u>cavalry</u> at the College, they made a precipate retreat....Col. Durfeys family have been staying with us for several days, as their yard...is the skirmishing ground & rifle balls are perforating the house a dozen times a day....Numbers*

A prewar photograph of Confederate brigadier general Henry A. Wise showing him as governor of Virginia. *Library of Congress.*

*& numbers of our poor people are camping out in the woods, fearful of the rifle balls, which are flying about in the streets, & of another shelling which may be inflicted on us at any moment....Only one shell struck the "old house" & that did not injure it all. I was in the library when it struck, just under the window sill - a fragment of shell. I have never felt the first sensation of fear since the enemy came in...& felt that if I was killed either by a musket ball when they were fighting just at our door, or by a shell, I should rejoin all I loved,-- there is joy ineffable in the thought.*

After occupying Williamsburg for a week, General Wise and his command found that the Federal troops showed no sign of attempting a major counterattack. Running low on provisions, he pulled his force out of Williamsburg and headed back to New Kent County. A few days later, Union troops quietly reentered the town and once again occupied Williamsburg. Now, however, more residents were gone, having taken the opportunity to flee "Northern oppression" and relocate to Richmond and other parts of the Confederacy. Those who remained could only hope and pray for the best.

# THE MARKET LINE

By 1863, Federal authorities were issuing rations to those who would come forward and swear an oath of allegiance to the United States. Many residents of Williamsburg refused, however, and the problem of feeding the city's population became a matter of some concern. To alleviate the situation, the Federal provost marshal established a "market line" on the Stage Road just west of the College of William & Mary. People living beyond the Federal lines north and west of the city were permitted to come in with farm produce to trade with the inhabitants. Wednesday became known as "Line Day."

At first, the "traders," who were mostly women, were allowed to mingle freely, but it was soon discovered that letters, newspapers and other prohibited articles were being passed back and forth. The provost marshal attempted to stop such activity by stretching two lengths of telegraph wire across the road and placing armed sentries between them. From then on, all trading was conducted across the wires under the guards' watchful eyes.

The wires, however, failed to deter the brisk business in contraband goods. It was noted by the officer in charge that a pretty face could distract a guard. Indeed, the women of the town boasted about their ability to smuggle letters and information through the lines on market days. Two ladies of Williamsburg were discovered attempting to smuggle goods under their hoop skirts. One unfortunate young miss was caught concealing letters in her sunbonnet. Others developed craftier and more successful methods. Letters could be hidden in jars of butter and jam or even dressed poultry. In

Confederate women smuggling quinine under a hoop skirt as shown in *Frank Leslie's Illustrated Newspaper*, 1863. *Author's collection.*

the right season, melons were plugged and secretly contained closely rolled letters and Richmond newspapers. Even official diplomatic correspondence and Confederate Secret Service documents passed through the market lines. Once in Williamsburg, any of these smuggled items could be mailed through the U.S. Post Office at Yorktown or Fort Monroe to any point in the world.

But the flow of information worked both ways. A woman with Union sympathies regularly passed Richmond newspapers and other intelligence— concealed in plugged watermelons—to Federal authorities. Whenever she appeared on Line Day, a Union officer would purchase her melons for his own table. After taking the melons to the provost marshal's office at the other end of town, the information was removed and forwarded to Fort Magruder, from where any valuable intelligence was telegraphed to Fort Monroe.

The market line not only served as a place to exchange goods and information but also as a meeting place for family and friends who found themselves separated by the divide between Union and Confederate grounds. Cynthia Coleman had originally decided to stay in town with her aged mother as Federal troops occupied the area in May 1862. She later slipped out of town, however, to be with her Confederate husband, who was serving as a hospital surgeon. After two years away, she attempted to re-enter town to visit her mother and sister in late 1864. Unhappily, she was refused entry. Afterward, she wrote of her experiences at "The Lines":

*I sent in to acquaint the Provost-Marshal with my vicinity and requested permission to visit my Mother. This was refused and I was denied the privilege of entering my own Town, but I was told my Mother and my friends might meet me at "The Lines." ...just above the College a thick wire was thrown and a sentinel posted to prevent passage to and fro. Here on a certain day in every week the country people were allowed to come and traffic with the people of the Town.*

On a snowy night in December 1864, Cynthia's mother, Lucy Tucker, and her sister Zettie traveled from their house on the Market Square to the market line to meet with Cynthia. Near the market line, there were several abandoned, roofless houses, where "the clouds of heaven flitting over looked in and dreary desolation sat at the vacant windows." Cynthia Coleman wrote:

*In one of these cheerless places we determined to keep our Christmas in the year 1864. The snow was falling fast, but we put up our umbrellas, kindled a fire, set on such logs as we could find, eat our cake and drank our toasts to our Confederate heroes in the hearing of the Sentinel whose forbearance we rewarded by giving him a glass of our wine, and then it was that he expressed his sympathy for us in a manly frank manner that touched us. Prisoners and Lunatics are grateful for very small favors.*

The market line continued until after General Lee's surrender at Appomattox in April 1865, when movement restrictions were relaxed and former Confederate soldiers were allowed to return home.

# "A Unique Entertainment"

During the summer of 1863, a new regiment of Union cavalry, the First New York Mounted Rifles, was ordered to Williamsburg to assume duties as provost guard in the town. The regiment had been mostly recruited from New York City and had served earlier that year in the operations around Suffolk, Virginia.

Major David Cronin of the regiment later wrote that the soldiers had experienced little contact with Southern civilians until their arrival in Williamsburg. Once in town, the more susceptible men flirted with "such small proportion of the fair sex as might condescend to notice a Yankee." One New Yorker attempted to explain to a young miss of the city that he was not a Yankee but had been born and bred in the Empire State. He explained that Yankees "were a species of New Englanders, something like gypsies." He further went on to say that he should be called a "York Shilling Folk" or "Albany Dutch," but not a Yankee. The young lady getting his attention replied, "Well, I would reckon you were a Yankee from your long palaver, though you may have a gypsy blend."

Notwithstanding the feeling of the women of the town toward the New Yorkers, an event occurred in July 1864 that united the town's inhabitants and the occupying soldiers. After the war, Major Cronin wrote an account of his military service around Williamsburg and recorded the incident:

> *A unique entertainment for our command, during July, was the witnessing of a marriage ceremony performed at the lines on the Richmond road. The ceremony was held there because all the churches in town were closed and*

*their pastors absentees. The Chaplain at the Fort was not acceptable to the contracting parties—not belonging to their denomination. Therefore, permission was given to a minister of their sect…to come to our lines on a certain morning and make the two one.*

The intended couple apparently made quite an unusual pair, and the proposed nuptials became a subject of great interest in Williamsburg. Cronin wrote that:

*The bride was about eighteen or twenty, good looking, rosy and plump. The groom was a widower…was over fifty, tall and thin with somewhat stooping shoulders. Neither was identified with the more aristocratic families of the town; yet the wide differences in their ages and the novelty of the circumstances under which the marriage was to be solemnized, aroused the greatest interest and curiosity among all classes of the inhabitants, eighty per cent of whom were women and well grown children.*

It was announced that because of the upcoming nuptials, restrictions on movement and gatherings would be relaxed, and any who wished might attend the ceremony at "the Lines." Consequently, on the appointed day, members of the most "exclusive families" turned out amongst the crowd of curious townspeople and Union soldiers. A minister from James City County was brought to the lines by Confederate cavalry scouts, who remained at a distance in the nearby woods, as eager to watch the proceedings as the townspeople. A fair-like atmosphere prevailed over all. Unfortunately, the one person not present was the bride, and then ensued an awkward wait.

A messenger was dispatched in search of her and returned with her answer, which was to "tell the old man if he don't stop hurrying me, I won't come at all." Suggesting that perhaps the prospective groom should fetch his bride, Major Cronin furnished the befuddled old man with a cavalry horse from one of his troopers. He then ordered a young lieutenant to accompany him and determine what the trouble was. After a short time, the lieutenant returned at a gallop and reported with a smile "that the bride was as skittish as a colt and positively refused to come to the altar." Following the lieutenant came the bridegroom. Calling upon Major Cronin to use his official authority as provost marshal in the town, the old man implored the major to go into town and order his young bride to the ceremony. By now, all of the guests and bystanders were alive with comments. Everyone wanted to know: "What, in goodness, is the matter with her?"

Major Cronin decided to personally ride into town to discover the answer. To his surprise, he found:

*The bride fully and tastefully arrayed, sitting on the porch between two bridesmaids, all languidly fanning themselves. She declared that she was not going to make a show of herself; that she had received no intimation that there were to be so many people on hand—all without invitation on her part; and finally she announced that she would never, never walk to the lines; that unless a carriage or some kind of conveyance were provided for her and her maids, she would not budge an inch.*

The bride's request presented Major Cronin with a quandary, for he knew of no transportation available in the town except for army ambulances at nearby Fort Magruder. After a further delay, the bridegroom managed to locate an old doctor's gig for which Major Cronin provided a horse. The bride and her bridesmaids were picked up, and finally, the wedding party set off:

*At length the bridal transport, moving slowly, came into view...the bride to be and her maids dressed in white, with parasols to match and all in the bloom of youth, presented a charming appearance. The groom and Lieutenant rode slightly in advance, the former a little awkwardly, as the stirrups were too short for him. Suddenly the whole procession halted. The groom rode back to the conveyance and we could see him bending over to listen to something the bride was saying. Then he dismounted and passing the reins to the lieutenant, strode rapidly towards us....He said, "She ordered me to get off that Yankee horse and walk on ahead; and now I am going to stay out of sight in the crowd, until I am called for."*

After their prolonged wait on the edge of town, the tired invited guests, the doubtful crowd of townspeople, the amused Union soldiers and the outlying Confederate cavalrymen got their unique entertainment. The couple stood together in the shade before the parson, and the ceremony went forward with no further delays. Everyone craned their necks to get a better view as the bride and groom were united as man and wife. Major Cronin ended his story by commenting, "It is said, despite predictions to the contrary, that the couple lived quite happily together as most married people do and survived for many years."

# THE LOST LIBRARY

Toward the end of 1863, Private Sam Putnam of the Twenty-Fifth Massachusetts Volunteers served on detached duty in Williamsburg and wrote to his father describing the condition of the town at this time:

> Most or rather a great many of the houses present the usual appearance of a captured town that is they look as if a "dose of salts had been through them" and they had been cleaned out. In one respect all Southern towns look alike, that air of neglect and decay hangs over them all, and Williamsburg is no exception.

Sadly for later historians, and no doubt to the distaste of Williamsburg's inhabitants, Putnam contributed to the "cleaning out" of the town. He went on to recount his part in ransacking a large library of old books and priceless historical documents:

> In a large house in town, near the headquarters of our section of our guard is a lot of books tumbled about promiscuously, all over the floor of one room evidently the library. I have borrowed two or three to—read you know. In the attic of this house which is a quaint old building "of the olden time" is a large lot of old letters, from many distinguished persons of the revolutionary time. I send you some one or more from Thos Jefferson—The sage of Monticello—This house was occupied at that time by one "Page" Lieutenant Governor of Virginia. You may find the letters of interest, there

*are one or two for the girls as they can see how the revolutionary maidens used to correspond. I'll send them all when I can. This house has been locked up since a day or two and we cannot go in again. The guard (Provost) is very strict in town, no one being allowed to go in without a pass....But I went in and borrowed a few books for all that I won't tell how. Ask me no questions and I tell you no lies. I shall try to send in this a letter from "Richard H. Lee" of the revolution. It seemed strange to be poking around among these musty records of the past and it was not wholly a spirit of curiosity that had possession of me at the time but more of reverence than any other, and I think you will rather prize the letters than otherwise.*

The "Lieutenant Governor" Putnam referred to was in fact Governor John Page from Gloucester County. He served as Virginia's chief executive from 1802 until 1805 and acquired quite an extensive library of books, correspondence and bound volumes of old copies of the *Virginia Gazette*. The house containing these historical artifacts belonged to Page's son-in-law, Robert Saunders, a professor at the College of William & Mary. On the morning that Union troops had entered Williamsburg, Saunders and his family had fled in such haste that they left their breakfast on the table.

Major Cronin of the First New York Mounted Rifles, serving as provost marshal of the town, was obviously unaware of Private Putnam's activities as he investigated the old house and library with an eye to saving what he could. Inspecting the premises with another officer, he wrote:

*Through age and neglect the building had become quite dilapidated in war time and the interior had been so often despoiled by indifferent soldiers that its library which had been one of the finest in Virginia had been completely wrecked. To preserve what was left of it the writer placed it under the special supervision of the patrols and prohibited further intrusion....We found the interior of the Page Mansion in a state of complete wreck...the former library in the most deplorable condition of disorder and ravage. In heaps on every side were half destroyed books, vellum-bound volumes, some of them with ornate toolings; letters and documents of all sorts, ragged files of precious colonial newspapers; torn folios of rare old engravings. With these were mingled the remains of shattered marble busts, fragments of ornamented book cases, window glass and plaster mixed with the mud from heavy boots of cavalrymen who seemed to have played football with everything of value in the place.*

Upon closer examination, the two Union officers discovered that they had stumbled upon an unexpected treasure of historic documents and lore:

> *In tipping over a broken chest in the garret to use as a seat, we picked up and examined some of its contents consisting wholly of old letters, bills of lading, rent receipts and jumbled manuscripts.... There were a couple of interesting letters signed by Meriwether Smith a member of the Continental Congress from Virginia, dated at Philadelphia about 1778, and giving an account of the foreign relations of the United Colonies. We found manuscript minutes of the secret sessions of the Congress, covering forty or fifty pages, consisting of memoranda of a debate upon the adoption of the American flag. We picked up a packet of receipts for rent of houses in Wmsburg, all signed "Geo Washington." There were about thirty of them....A thick packet of letters were from Thomas Jefferson to Page, some dating from their college days, others written when Jefferson was the American Minister in Paris. Other letters were equally interesting and precious, such as one from Count Pulaski offering his service to the State of Virginia; several from Richard Henry Lee, in one of which he announced the capture of Major General Charles Lee and the suspicions aroused by it; two or three were from Martha Washington to Mrs. Page and numbers were from Madison, Arthur Lee, Peyton Randolph and other of the most prominent characters of the Revolution.*

To be sure, there are many present-day historians who would have given anything to be present with Major Cronin that day. In an effort to salvage the rapidly disintegrating library, Major Cronin prevailed upon Captain Brown, the acting assistant adjutant at nearby Fort Magruder:

> *[T]he following day the Captain sent to town an army wagon accompanied by infantrymen with shovels. The litter of garret and library was conveyed to the Fort where a number of ladies belonging to the families of officers assisted in carefully looking over the miscellaneous mass discovering many more relics of value nearly all of which, I was afterward informed, reached public historical collections as gifts.*

Regardless of Major Cronin's and Captain Brown's good intentions, none of the contents of the lost library were properly accounted for. It is to be hoped that Private Putnam's family truly did "prize" the letters they received, because it seems they were the last to ever see them. The letters, along with the rest of Governor Page's library, have disappeared and never been recovered.

# WISTAR'S RAID

A seemingly unconnected series of events culminating in the failure of an attempt to free Union prisoners of war and kidnap the Confederate president, Jefferson Davis, had their beginnings in Williamsburg in late 1863 with the murder of a newly appointed Federal provost marshal.

Since Williamsburg's occupation in May 1862, the city had been under martial law. The provost marshal was charged with governing the city and maintaining the Federal occupation. On October 6, 1863, the office was given to Lieutenant William W. Disosway, a handsome, intelligent young man of nineteen years of age. Although he was still young, he was an experienced soldier, having served as a sergeant in the First New York "Lincoln" Cavalry in the campaigns of the Army of the Potomac. Commissioned in the field, he now belonged to the First New York Mounted Rifles. Unhappily, his career as a provost marshal would only last about a week.

On October 13, Lieutenant Disosway was reading a newspaper on the steps of the provost marshal's office located at the Vest House on the east end of town. There, he was interrupted by a corporal's guard escorting a prisoner, Private William Boyle. Boyle had drunkenly tried to force his way into Williamsburg past a guard post and been arrested for disorderly conduct. Still holding his newspaper, Disosway interviewed Private Boyle from the steps.

After hearing the facts of Boyle's arrest, Lieutenant Disosway ordered that the private should be taken back to camp with instructions that he was to return, sober, in the morning. It was at this instant that Boyle,

The Vest House served as headquarters for generals of both sides and was later the Federal Provost Marshal's office. *Special Collections, John D. Rockefeller Jr. Library, Colonial Williamsburg Foundation.*

who, surprisingly, had not been disarmed, pulled out his service revolver and threatened to shoot the lieutenant. The adjacent guards immediately leveled their muskets at Boyle, but the brave lieutenant attempted to calm the situation by ordering them not to fire. As Disosway moved toward Boyle with the intent to disarm him, Boyle fired his revolver. The young provost marshal was hit in the mouth and died instantly. As his body dropped to the ground, there was a brief scuffle as Boyle was quickly overpowered and belatedly disarmed by the guards. He was removed for imprisonment at nearby Fort Magruder, and Lieutenant Disosway's body was taken to the local undertaker.

The next day saw an impressive military funeral at nearby Fort Magruder. The entire command was present, and several women of Williamsburg sent flowers to show their sympathy for the untimely death of the youthful lieutenant. He had apparently charmed the ladies of the town in his brief time there. Four Union officers were assigned to be an escort for Disosway's remains as they were returned to the North.

Private Boyle was placed under confinement at the small military jail at Fort Magruder. Tried for murder by a military court-martial, he was quickly found guilty and sentenced to be hanged. As required, the proceedings of the court were sent to the judge advocate general in Washington for approval of the sentence; they made their way to President Lincoln's desk. There, they waited for the president's signature to finalize the matter.

Meanwhile, Major General Benjamin F. Butler arrived at Fort Monroe in Hampton in November 1863 to take over the command of the Department of Virginia and North Carolina. A political general from Massachusetts, Butler was a controversial figure. While in command at Fort Monroe in 1861, he had proclaimed that slaves who had run away from the Confederate lines and come under his protection were "contraband of war," thus forcing United States policy on the matter. In June 1861, his forces had engaged in the first real land battle with the rebels at Big Bethel. The next year, during the occupation of New Orleans, he hanged a civilian who had desecrated a U.S. flag and threatened to label the ladies of the city as prostitutes if they insulted his soldiers, earning the title "Beast Butler" from outraged Confederates.

Now, in late 1863, as he returned to Virginia and assumed his new command, Butler looked toward the presidential election of 1864. As a war Democrat with aspirations for the White House, he needed a military success to perhaps influence the upcoming Democratic convention in his favor. An opportunity presented itself when Colonel Robert M. West, military governor of the Williamsburg area and commander at Fort Magruder, communicated a secret plan to Brigadier General Isaac J. Wistar at Yorktown.

West felt that the time was right for a rapid cavalry raid on the Confederate capital at Richmond from the direction of Williamsburg. It was thought that with General Robert E. Lee's main army being in Northern Virginia, the Richmond defenses would be weakened. Intelligence sources suggested that although there was always Confederate cavalry in the area, there was, at present, no sizable rebel force between Williamsburg and Richmond, a distance of only about forty miles. If a force of raiders could get into Richmond quickly, they could free the Union prisoners of war at the infamous Libby Prison and Belle Isle, then possibly destroy factories and rebel supplies before the surprised Confederates could react.

While inspecting his new command, Butler conferred with General Wistar at Yorktown concerning the feasibility of such a raid. Here was the opportunity Butler sought. In one stroke, he could advance both his military career and political future. After receiving approval for their proposed

*Left*: Major General Benjamin Butler. *Library of Congress.*

*Right*: Brigadier General Isaac J. Wister. *Wikimedia Commons.*

operation, Wistar and West began making their preparations. Troops began to move and quietly assemble near Williamsburg.

Departing the Federal lines at Williamsburg early on the morning of February 6, 1864, General Wistar commanded about seven thousand infantry and cavalry, including three black regiments. His plan called for a rapid dash across nearby New Kent County to quickly capture the Confederate pickets at Bottoms Bridge on the Chickahominy River, the eastern approach to the Confederate capital in Richmond. Then, his cavalry would make a swift thrust into the city, where they would divide into several smaller groups.

Once in Richmond, a detachment of 250 men from the Eleventh Pennsylvania Cavalry would destroy the Confederate navy yard at Rockett's Landing on the James River. Troops from the Third New York Cavalry were to liberate the prisoners at Libby Prison and Belle Isle, burning the city's bridges over the James River as they returned. Still other detachments would deploy to destroy the Central Railroad Depot and tear up as much track as time permitted. Finally, Major James Wheelan, with 300 men of the First New York Mounted Rifles, would ride straight to the Confederate White House at Twelfth and Marshall Streets, where they would capture the Confederate president, Jefferson Davis. With the prisoner in hand, they would return to Bottoms Bridge, followed by the rest of the raiders. By that time, the slower-moving infantry support would have arrived, and the entire force would fall back to Williamsburg.

After quickly moving up the Virginia peninsula, the raiders made good time and arrived at Bottoms Bridge ahead of the projected schedule. Once they made it there, however, General Wistar's plan began to unravel. He discovered that the Confederates were expecting him. Instead of the usual guard of about twenty soldiers, Wistar found a strong entrenched rebel force of infantry, cavalry and artillery. In addition, the defenders seemingly knew that the Union soldiers were coming. They had removed the planks of the bridge to prevent a crossing.

After scouting around both sides of the bridge, no ford over the Chickahominy River could be located, so Wistar ordered Major Wheelan and his Mounted Rifles to attempt to force a crossing at the bridge with a frontal assault. It proved to be useless, however, as the Northern horsemen were repulsed, with nine men killed or wounded. The distant sounds of trains arriving with more Confederate reinforcements from Richmond decided the matter, as it was apparent that the element of surprise had been lost. Left with no choice, General Wistar ended the operation and retreated to Williamsburg.

Back in Williamsburg, it was learned from Confederate newspapers that the Richmond authorities had suspected a raid for some weeks and known of the actual operation for several days. According to the papers, a Yankee deserter had furnished the information.

It seems that while Private Boyle was waiting for his execution at Williamsburg to be approved by President Lincoln, he had talked one of his guards into helping him escape. Four days before the expedition, Boyle's guard had filed off his manacles. After escaping his confinement, Boyle immediately slipped across the lines into the Confederacy and made his way to Richmond. When he was arrested by Confederate authorities, he told them everything he knew about the Federal forces around Williamsburg, including the fact that preparations for a large raid were in progress. Already suspicious, the Confederates had moved quickly to reinforce and strengthen defensive positions on the approaches to Richmond.

Thus, General Wistar's raid ended in failure, and with it went Benjamin Butler's aspirations for military glory and a presidential nomination. In November, President Lincoln was re-elected, defeating another Democrat, General George B. McClellan.

Curiously, the day after Wistar's troops returned, 109 Union prisoners held at Libby Prison in Richmond made their way through a tunnel and escaped into the city. The Confederate authorities quickly recaptured most of them, but a few made it through the lines and arrived at Williamsburg. There, they were greeted by the same cavalrymen who, just a few days prior, had tried to free them. About three weeks after Wistar's expedition, another Union raid on Richmond under Brigadier General Judson Kilpatrick was attempted on the authorization of President Lincoln. It also ended in failure.

As for the deserter and murderer, Private Boyle was initially held by the Confederates and once again imprisoned. General Butler, angered by both Boyle's escape and his complicity with the rebels, offered to exchange any number of Confederate prisoners for him but was refused. Eventually, Boyle was released and disappeared into history. Rumor has it that he was later killed in a western mining accident, but one of his former comrades from the Mounted Rifles reported seeing him in New York City after the war.

As for Private Thomas Abraham of the 139th New York Volunteers, the hapless guard who had assisted Boyle in his escape, he was arrested, placed in close confinement and treated to his own court-martial. Found guilty and sentenced to death, his sentence, unlike Boyle's, was swiftly carried out. On March 7, 1864, Private Abraham was executed at Yorktown.

# THE DOCTOR IN BLUE

A t least one visitor to Williamsburg during the war was well regarded by the people of the town even though he wore the hated Union blue.

Born into a distinguished Philadelphia family in 1823, Peter Wager received a better-than-average education as a young man. Through family connections, he received an appointment to the U.S. Navy as a midshipman at the age of sixteen. He served in the East and West Indies, patrolled for slave ships between Africa and Brazil and fought native islanders in the Pacific. During the Mexican War, he patrolled off the Mexican coast and served onshore with the Naval Brigade at the bombardment and siege of Vera Cruz in 1847.

Unfortunately for his career, he seemed to have made some enemies. He was charged with several counts of misconduct and suddenly dropped from the Naval Rolls in 1855. Upon moving back near family in Pennsylvania, he chose a new profession. He attended medical school at the University of Pennsylvania and graduated just as the Civil War began.

Upon joining the army, Dr. Wager was commissioned as an assistant surgeon and found himself assigned to the Fifth Pennsylvania Cavalry in early 1862. Initially, he was concerned with the care of Confederate wounded who remained in the city after the Battle of Williamsburg, but he soon found himself charged with a more difficult task.

The Eastern State Lunatic Asylum, located on the southeast end of town, had become a thorny problem for the occupying forces. The hospital was an institution of the State of Virginia, but with the occupation of the town and the unfortunate death of the superintendent, Dr. John Minson Galt, state authorities were unable to discharge their responsibilities. In short, the patients were left without proper care.

To further compound matters, Federal authorities had tentatively dismissed several "disloyal" employees and replaced them with several persons who swore their allegiance to the United States. They, in turn, abandoned their duties and fled Williamsburg in August 1862, when it seemed as though the Confederates might reoccupy the city. Regardless of the threat, Williamsburg remained under Federal control, but once again, the mental patients found themselves without care or even food.

On August 21, 1862, the town provost marshal, Colonel David Campbell, assigned Dr. Wager as the superintendent and physician-in-charge of the asylum. Dr. Wager quickly took to his new role. With a small staff of army hospital stewards supplemented by several former employees (whom he rehired regardless of their allegiance), Dr. Wager requisitioned the necessary food and medicines from the U.S. Quartermaster and soon had the hospital efficiently running. About this time, another Federal surgeon referred to Dr. Wager as "a very accomplished, middle-aged gentleman."

Dr. Wager became a special friend of Sallie Galt, whose late brother had been the last superintendent. She, in turn, lent Dr. Wager books from her brother's library on the care of the mentally ill. He became an advocate of "moral management," the idea that mental patients should be treated humanely and with respect.

When Confederate forces raided Williamsburg in April 1863, he offered the people of the town sanctuary at the hospital. He not only protected them from the skirmishing in the streets and the shelling of the town but "welcomed them with a feast of coffee." During the raid, however, Dr. Wager found himself a prisoner of Confederate general Henry Wise but was instructed and allowed to keep caring for his patients. He protested the Confederate removal of the hospital's food supplies and found himself ordered to return to his own lines, leaving the hospital to the Confederates. After their departure several days later, he returned once again to resume his duties, bringing along fresh rations.

As if his compassion for the hospital patients was not enough, Dr. Wager took it upon himself to provide medical care to the town's residents. He also recognized the historical significance of the old colonial capital. He tried—in vain—to stop the destruction of the two remaining outbuildings of the royal governor's palace, but he did succeed in having the eighteenth-century statue of Lord Botetourt removed from the seemingly constant fighting around the burned-out ruins of the Wren Building at the College of William & Mary. On his own authority, he had it brought to the asylum for storage and safekeeping in March 1865.

As much as he was admired, Dr. Wager had a not-so-secret failing—he was too fond of the bottle. Several times during his tenure as superintendent, it was noted by residents of the town that he was "incapacitated." Still, he did manage to care for his patients.

Dr. Wager remained in charge of the asylum for almost eight months after General Lee had surrendered at Appomattox. As Federal troops were withdrawn from the city proper in September 1865, a newly appointed state board of directors insisted that they be given control of the hospital. Fearing for the care of his patients, Dr. Wager refused to relinquish control until being ordered to turn over the hospital on November 1.

Installation of memorial stone for Dr. Peter Wager at Bruton Parish Church, 2015. *Author's collection.*

Although he was no longer associated with the hospital, he stayed in Williamsburg after being assigned as the surgeon responsible for Federal troops still at Fort Magruder. He held that post until Christmas Day, 1868, when he died in Williamsburg.

The *U.S. Registers of Deaths in the Regular Army* listed the cause of his death as "Not Stated," but perhaps it involved his intemperance. Bruton Parish Church records declare his cause of death as "nervous exhaustion." Whatever the reason, several ladies of the town took it upon themselves to lay Dr. Wager to rest in the Episcopal churchyard. He was buried during a small ceremony on December 27, with Reverend Thomas Ambler officiating. The only persons present were all former Confederates, but they had valued the presence of U.S. army surgeon Dr. Peter Wager in their town.

His burial remained relatively unknown until 2014. At that time, the fact that he was buried in the churchyard was "rediscovered." Regrettably, there was no gravestone. Research indicated the approximate location of his remains, and the Williamsburg Battlefield Association made it a priority to place a memorial stone there. In 2015, this was accomplished, and Dr. Wager can now once again be remembered for his time in Williamsburg.

# The Picket Post

Private Austin Gannon stamped his feet to warm them as he contemplated his post. He was on picket duty on the western end of Williamsburg near the College of William & Mary. A member of Battery D, Sixteenth New York Volunteer Artillery, he had been assigned to the reserve guard for one of the picket posts on the Old Stage Road (now called Richmond Road), which led west to Richmond.

It was three o'clock in the morning on February 11, 1865. The Civil War had been raging across America for almost four years. As General Ulysses S. Grant laid siege to Richmond and General William Sherman was moving through the Carolinas after having cut his way through Georgia, the Southern Confederacy was almost finished. But on this dark, cold night, the war must have seemed far off to Private Gannon.

The rebel guerrillas who harassed the occupying Federal soldiers hadn't been active in the immediate area for some time other than keeping the town under observation. There had not been a serious raid on Williamsburg for almost two years. Nonetheless, Union troops had been busy fortifying the area around the college. One resident later reminisced:

> In order to afford protection against frequent Confederate raids, the windows and doors of the College, opening to the north and westward were bricked up, with port holes in them for small arms. Deep ditches were dug from the north, east, and the southeast corners of the College, extending some distance beyond the "Stage Road," and the "Mill Road." In these ditches

*were placed vertically big logs ten feet long, and three feet in the ground.*
*These logs were fitted with port holes so as to guard against Cavalry raids*
*down the two roads. Some distance in the rear of the College and extending*
*in a curved line far beyond the Mill and Stage roads was constructed an*
*abatis consisting of tops of big oak and beech trees with sharpened limbs set*
*in the ground, standing westward and all entangled with wire.*

Perhaps Private Gannon was thinking of the war he was missing by being on guard duty in a backwater Southern town. Maybe he was thinking of home back in New York. Or maybe he just wanted to get back to a warm bed. Whatever was on his mind that night came quickly to an end as a group of riders approached his picket post.

An outlying Northern sentry called out a challenge to the mounted men who appeared to be dressed in Union blue. When he received no reply, the Federal soldier nervously fingered the trigger of his weapon. As the unknown riders kept coming, he raised his weapon and attempted to fire, but the weapon failed. Retreating back to the reserve force where Private Gannon and the other pickets were waiting, the sentry suddenly found himself chased by wildly screaming Confederate raiders.

The next few moments were a blur of confusion on the dark road. Private Gannon and the rest of the reserve guard scattered in disorder as the Confederate horsemen dashed down the road shooting to the left and right. Quickly, the Confederates captured four horses and left the way they came.

As the alarm spread, Union cavalrymen assembled and rode out to try to find the raiders, but they had disappeared into the black night. The town was in an uproar as the sleepy residents looked out to see what all the excitement was about.

A bit later, the Union pickets would learn that they had faced rangers from Colonel John S. Mosby's Forty-Third Battalion of Virginia Cavalry. Known as the "Gray Ghost," Mosby and his men had frustrated Federal troops in Northern Virginia for some time. A small group of Mosby's men, commanded by Captain Thomas W.T. Richards, had been assigned the task of probing the Williamsburg line. The mission had been given to Colonel Mosby by no less than Confederate general Robert E. Lee. With the tightening siege of Richmond and Petersburg in progress, Lee's intent was to test the Federal forces' preparedness on the lower Virginia peninsula.

With this raid, General Lee learned that the local Union garrison was not expecting any movement in their direction. Unfortunately, he could not use the information to his advantage. In less than two months, Lee would be forced to abandon the Confederate capital at Richmond. A week after that, he surrendered the remnants of his army at Appomattox on April 9, 1865, ending the war in Virginia.

Unfortunately for Private Gannon, this meant nothing that night. During those few hectic minutes on the Old Stage Road, he was shot dead by one of the raiders. Along with four wounded Federal soldiers, Private Austin Gannon of the Sixteenth New York Volunteer Artillery was among the last wartime casualties in Williamsburg.

# Epilogue

With the surrender of Confederate general Robert E. Lee and his Army of Northern Virginia at Appomattox in April 1865, an uneasy peace returned to Williamsburg and the surrounding area. An office of the Bureau of Refugees, Freedmen, and Abandoned Lands (or "Freedmen's Bureau") opened in town. Later, a Quaker mission was set up at Fort Magruder. With the end of hostilities and the departure of some of the local Federal troops, female missionaries arrived from Philadelphia and took up residence in the fort. They immediately opened a school to teach former slaves in the area to read and write.

Although the shooting had stopped, and their numbers were reduced through demobilization, Federal troops continued to occupy Williamsburg. It was not until September 1865 that the last of them departed the city proper. However, Federal soldiers remained at Yorktown and around the Williamsburg area for another five years, until Virginia formally rejoined the Union in January 1870. Until that time, under Reconstruction, Williamsburg, along with the rest of Virginia, was part of Military District Number 1.

Cynthia Coleman, upon finally returning to her home after three years of exile, remembered:

> *The houses were torn to pieces and the bricks carried away. When the owners returned after the War the foundations alone remained of what had once been abodes of comfort. With the year that followed the surrender at Appomattox the old people, deprived of hope, weary with the march of life,*

Postwar view of the Duke of Gloucester Street, Williamsburg's main thoroughfare, showing how the town looked shortly after the war ended. *Special Collections, John D. Rockefeller Jr. Library, Colonial Williamsburg Foundation.*

View of the Williamsburg Courthouse after the war ended. *Colonial Williamsburg Foundation.*

*abandoned the struggle, crossed their pale hands and lay down to die, as effectually killed by the results of the War as if they had fallen on the field of battle.*

In April 1865, Captain Robert Anderson Bright came home to Williamsburg, his birthplace. Educated at a private boys' school in the town, then at the College of William & Mary and, finally, at the University of Virginia, he had he joined the Peninsula Light Artillery in May 1861. Only twenty-one years of age, he subsequently served in the Thirty-Second Virginia Infantry and was on the staff of Major General George Pickett by 1863. Slightly wounded at Gettysburg, he was a witness to the climax of "Pickett's Charge." He ended the war on April 9, 1865, when he surrendered with Lee at Appomattox.

After Captain Bright's return to Williamsburg, he was always proud to boast that he was a Confederate veteran but also seemed willing to help the nation come back together. A few months after Appomattox, he happened to read a statement made by the secretary of the treasury in which it was shown that because of the war, the national debt was several billion dollars. The total cost ran to twelve figures, ending with twenty-five cents. According to the account of his son, Robert S. Bright,

*My father put a 25 cent note in a letter to the Secretary of the Treasury in which he said he had just returned from the war, that he had been re-constructed sooner than most of his compatriots, that he had seen from the Secretary's statement the awful debt he had helped to make the government contract and he wished to make what amends he could for his part in that, and he therefore sent a sum sufficient to cut off two figures of the national debt, trusting that he would find five other as patriotic Americans to tackle the other ten, and signed it "Ex-Confederate Officer."*

No resident of Williamsburg remained untouched by the Civil War. Some dwelled on what they had lost and mourned the dead Confederacy. Others, while remaining true to their beliefs, tried to make the most of the situation. All in Williamsburg who lived through the war would never forget their various experiences.

# RESIDENTS OF WILLIAMSBURG, 1860

| #. Name | Age | Sex | Race | Occupation |
|---------|-----|-----|------|------------|
| 1. Rebecca JONES | 50 | F | | |
| 2. E.H. LIVELY | 25 | M | | Editor |
| Mary A. | 40 | F | | |
| Robert A. | 20 | M | | Printer |
| Mary F. | 25 | F | | |
| 3. Henley T. JONES Sr. | 45 | M | | Farmer |
| Mary A.H. | 39 | F | | |
| Martha H. | 20 | F | | |
| Henley T. Jr. | 18 | M | | |
| S. Hunter | 16 | F | | |
| Wm. S. | 14 | M | | |
| Daniel S. | 10 | M | | |
| Cornelia M. | 8 | F | | |
| Allen B. | 3 | M | | |
| Binny(?) | 9 mos. | F | | |

APPENDIX A

| #. Name | Age | Sex | Race | Occupation |
|---|---|---|---|---|
| 4. A.G. SOUTHALL | 50 | M | | Statuary |
| Virginia T.F. | 44 | F | | |
| Travis | 22 | M | | |
| Mary F. | 21 | F | | |
| Elizabeth B. | 14 | F | | |
| Cate H. | 11 | F | | |
| Jennie A. | 9 | F | | |
| 5. Sally GRESHAM | 53 | F | | |
| Mat. ASHBY | 29 | M | Mulatto | Shoemaker |
| Elizabeth STEWARD | 27 | F | Mulatto | |
| Wm. H. Steward | 10 | M | Mulatto | |
| Amanda SIMPSON | 13 | F | Black | |
| 6. Francis PHILLIPS | 50 | M | | Engineer |
| Sarah Phillips | 25 | F | | |
| Francis S. | 9 | M | | |
| Sally B. | 7 | F | | |
| Lucy J. | 6 | F | | |
| Andrew F. | 4 | M | | |
| Joseph | 2 | M | | |
| 7. Sydney FURGERSON | 66 | F | | |
| 8. Sarah LINDSAY | 26 | F | | |
| Mary W. WARE | 17 | F | | |
| Annie B. SUNDAY | 8 | F | | |
| Edmond B. | 5 | M | | |
| Patty JONES | 80 | F | Black | Servant |
| 9. Susan DODD | 18 | F | | Seamstress |
| Sally PIERCE | 35 | F | | Dress Maker |

| #. Name | Age | Sex | Race | Occupation |
|---|---|---|---|---|
| 10. Catherine WILLSON | 38 | F | | Tayloress |
| Delarson(?) MAHONE | 25 | M | | Shoemaker |
| Able Mahone | 18 | M | | |
| 11. John MAHONE | 53 | M | | Shopkeeper |
| Susan | 51 | F | | |
| Walter | 17 | M | | |
| Alex | 9 | M | | |
| 12. Joshua DAVIS | 26 | M | | Mechanic |
| S.E. | 19 | F | | |
| Sinn(?) | 1 | M | | |
| Courtney Davis | 16 | F | Black | |
| 13. Mary TILLEDGE | 51 | F | | Seamstress |
| John C. | 16 | M | | |
| William T. | 14 | M | | |
| 14. Mary S. HUNT | 42 | F | | Confectionary |
| E.I. | 20 | F | | |
| M.E. | 18 | F | | |
| Julia | 15 | F | | |
| Cornelius | 10 | M | | |
| Exony(?) | 8 | F | | |
| Sesttia(?) | 5 | F | | |
| James MAHONE | 19 | M | | Officer at Asylum |
| 15. Mary ARMFIELD | 50 | F | Black | Wash woman |
| Sally Simpson | 40 | F | Black | Wash woman |
| Parker P. CUSTIS | 3 | M | Black | |

| #. Name | Age | Sex | Race | Occupation |
|---|---|---|---|---|
| 16. Celia MULATTOLEN | 25 | F | | Merchant |
| Florence L. | 9 | F | | |
| Edward | 8 | M | | |
| Cornelia | 6 | F | | |
| Janera(?) | 6 mos. | F | | |
| 17. Sommersette MOORE | 46 | M | | Master Shoe Maker |
| Alice BALEY | 63 | F | | |
| Georgianna CLARK | 45 | F | | Mantua maker |
| 18. John T. JAMES | 60 | M | | Master Mechanic |
| Celina E. James | 50 | F | | |
| Elizabeth James | 30 | F | | |
| Martha James | 25 | F | | Teacher |
| Henry James | 16 | M | | |
| 19. A J.(?) HOFHEIMER | 33 | M | | Merchant |
| Rachel | 25 | F | | |
| Henry C. | 3 | M | | |
| Cora | 1 | F | | |
| Polly CHRISTOPHER | 20 | F | Mulatto | Servant |
| 20. John W. HUTCHINGS | 50 | M | | Merchant |
| 21. Martha BOWERY | 50 | F | | Seamstress |
| Virginia | 19 | F | | Seamstress |
| Lucy | 17 | F | | Seamstress |
| Lemuel | 14 | M | | |
| 22. Anne JAMES | 35 | F | Black | Washerwoman |
| 23. Neal(?) Ryass(?) | 67 | M | Black | Fisherman |

| #. Name | Age | Sex | Race | Occupation |
|---|---|---|---|---|
| 24. Robert F. Cole | 41 | M | | Farmer real estate |
| Elizabeth | 31 | F | | |
| Robert R. | 12 | M | | |
| Jesse | 11 | M | | |
| Edward R. | 9 | M | | |
| Denison | 6 | M | | |
| Ella C. NEVILLE | 18 | F | | |
| 25. Lemuel J. BOWDEN | 45 | M | | Lawyer |
| Martha E. | 43 | F | | |
| T.R. | 19 | M | | |
| L.G. | 15 | M | | |
| Mary A. | 13 | F | | |
| 26. Mildred BOWDEN | 75 | F | | |
| 27. Archer BROOKS | 28 | M | | Master plasterer |
| Margarett | 22 | F | | |
| Leanna | 5 | F | | |
| Archer, Jr. | 3 | M | | |
| Wm. M. | 1 | M | | |
| Wm. AWFIELD(?) | 14 | M | Black | Servant |
| 28. James T. MAHONE | 28 | M | | Carpenter |
| Susan H. | 27 | F | | |
| John D. | 4 | M | | |
| Jms H. | 3 | M | | |
| Anne B. | 1 | F | | |
| Jennie DAVIS | 17 | F | Black | Servant |

| #. Name | Age | Sex | Race | Occupation |
|---|---|---|---|---|
| 29. Becky DAVIS | 55 | F | Black | Washerwoman |
| Hennetta | 25 | F | Black | Washerwoman |
| 30. Levinia C. MINOR | 38 | F | | |
| Clara M. | 12 | F | | |
| Lucian | 7 | M | | |
| Eliza W | 6 | F | | |
| Ferrel(?) | 2 | M | | |
| 31. Wm. R. DAVIS | 32 | M | | Farmer |
| Jane E. | 22 | F | | |
| Maryetta | 5 | F | | |
| Frech(?) | 3 | M | | |
| Isabella J. | 1 | F | | |
| Wm CORTS(?) | 10 | M | Mulatto | Servant |
| 32. Horace MOORE | 52 | M | | Mechanic |
| Maria | 51 | | | |
| Orlando BALL | 22 | M | | Mechanic |
| Susan E. | 18 | F | | |
| 33. Elizabeth DAVIS | 80 | F | | |
| 34. Richard A. CHRISTIAN | 38 | M | | Public Officer |
| Martha | 38 | F | | |
| Jhn. M. Rudd | 19 | M | | |
| Bettie A. | 16 | F | | |
| Henry | 13 | M | | |
| Molly A. Christian | 7 | F | | |
| Pattie J. | 5 | F | | |
| Martha BLANTON | 18 | F | Mulatto | House Servant |

| #. Name | Age | Sex | Race | Occupation |
|---|---|---|---|---|
| 35. Jerry(?) BUNTING | 32 | M | | Postmaster |
| Mary A. | 25 | F | | |
| Thos. LINDSAY | 58 | M | | Blacksmith |
| Jane F. | 20 | F | | School Teacher |
| Ella ___ | 15 | F | | |
| George | 10 | M | | |
| O.J. Bunting | 9 | M | | |
| Caroline | 5 | F | | |
| Marietta | 4 | F | | |
| Infant not named | 1 | M | | |
| 36. Catherine M. MAUPIN | 40 | F | | |
| Wm. H.E. MORECOCK | 23 | M | | Clerk |
| Sarah M. Maupin | 19 | F | | |
| Saml. J. Maupin | 16 | M | | |
| Jno. M. | 14 | M | | |
| Jessee G. | 13 | M | | |
| 37. Leroy RANDOLPH | 32 | M | Mulatto | Barber |
| 38. Jno. W. CLOWES | 27 | M | | Master Mechanic |
| Elizabeth | 23 | F | | |
| Eugene H. | 1 | M | | |
| Emma JAMES | 12 | F | Black | Servant |
| 39. John S. CHARLES | 45 | M | | Shoemaker |
| Elizabeth | 61 | F | | |
| Julia A. | 45 | F | | |
| Elizabeth G. | 15 | F | | |
| Maria | 9 | F | | |
| Jno. S.C. Charles Jr. | 7 | M | | |

| #. Name | Age | Sex | Race | Occupation |
|---|---|---|---|---|
| Julia L. | 5 | F | | |
| Infant not named | 1 mos. | | | |
| 40. Talbot SWEENEY | 30 | M | | Lawyer |
| Mary E. | 53 | F | | |
| 41. Alex. DUNLOP | 43 | M | Black | |
| June(?) STEWARD | 75 | F | Black | |
| 42. Robt. BARHAM | 31 | M | | Mechanic |
| W.(?) J. | 26 | F | | |
| Thos. P. | 5 | M | | |
| Robt. H. | 3 | M | | |
| 43. Jno. S. HAZELGROVE | 39 | M | | Merchant |
| Susannah S. | 35 | F | | |
| Josephine | 9 | F | | |
| Virginia | 6 | F | | |
| Louisa | 3 | F | | |
| 44. Tom CRAWLEY | 40 | M | Black | Carpenter |
| Lucy | 40 | F | Mulatto | |
| Emily CUMBER | 14 | F | Mulatto | |
| 45. Cornellia M. JONES | 32 | F | | |
| Isabella C. | 10 | F | | |
| Mary E. | 8 | F | | |
| Ida C. | 5 | F | | |
| 46. Robert SAUNDERS | 55 | M | | Farmer |
| Lucy B. | 53 | F | | |
| Letia(?) L. | 21 | F | | |
| Robela(?) | 16 | F | | |

| #. Name | Age | Sex | Race | Occupation |
|---|---|---|---|---|
| Robt. L.P. | 15 | M | | |
| Barbara PAGE | 59 | F | | |
| 47. Lucy A. DOUGLAS | 47 | F | | |
| Joan E. | 18 | F | | |
| Molly B. | 16 | F | | |
| Lucy A. | 13 | F | | |
| Jno. B. | 11 | M | | |
| Jimmie(?) M.(?) | 9 | M | | |
| Robt. B. | 7 | M | | |
| Wm. R.C. | 50 | M | | Public Officer |
| 48. Sydney SMITH | 38 | M | | Lawyer |
| Virginia | 30 | F | | |
| Alva(?) E. | 11 | M | | |
| Martha L. | 9 | F | | |
| Virginia B. | 7 | F | | |
| Henry | 5 | M | | |
| Cora B. | 3 | F | | |
| Sydney | 1 | M | | |
| 49. G.R. HARWOOD | 25 | M | | Harness maker |
| Sarah | 26 | F | | |
| Tabitha | 50 | F | | |
| Florence | 6 mos. | | | |
| 50. Thos. J.L. SNEAD | 28 | M | | Prof of Mathematics |
| 51. Chas. W. Coleman | 32 | M | | Physician |
| F.C. | 62 | F | | |
| Hellen M. | 26 | F | | |
| Thos. C. CARRINGTON | 21 | M | | Farmer |

| #. Name | Age | Sex | Race | Occupation |
|---|---|---|---|---|
| 52. Jno. M. KIDD | 28 | M | | Merchant Tailor |
| Elizabeth R. | 21 | F | | |
| Jane | 49 | F | | |
| Joseph QUASE(?) | 35 | M | | Tailor |
| Chas. S. LANGDON | 17 | M | | Apprentice Tailor |
| 53. Richd. W. BIDGOOD | 47 | M | | Dentist personal |
| Joseph V. | 19 | M | | |
| 54. Tanner CAPPS | 44 | M | | Tailor |
| Fanny Doudgh(?) | 48 | F | | Seamstress |
| Julia A. Capps | 23 | F | | Tailoress |
| Fanny BADKINS | 6 | F | | |
| Sally Capps | 3 mos. | | | |
| 55. Margarett PAISERIS/ PARSONS(?) | 90 | F | Mulatto | |
| Julia MINSON | 16 | F | Mulatto | Seamstress |
| 56. John A. DENEUFVILLE | 67 | M | | Merchant |
| H.F. | 50 | F | | |
| M.M. | 21 | F | | |
| Thomas | 18 | M | Black | House Servant |
| 57. John COKE | 63 | M | | Farmer |
| Eliza | 58 | F | | |
| Octavious | 21 | M | | Lawyer |
| John A. | 17 | M | | |
| 58. Wm. H. YERBY | 45(?) | M | | Clerk of the Court |
| R.J.H. | 7 | M | | |
| Mary L. Yerby | 1 | F | | |

| #. Name | Age | Sex | Race | Occupation |
|---|---|---|---|---|
| 59. Rachel SCOTT | 45 | F | Mulatto | Washerwoman |
| 60. Jno(?) D. MUNTFORD | 49 | M | | Farmer |
| Margaret | 40 | F | | |
| Maria | 18 | F | | |
| Sally | 16 | F | | |
| Nannie | 14 | F | | |
| John | 12 | M | | |
| Beverly | 3 | M | | |
| 61. Thomas MOORE | 23 | M | | Farmer |
| 62. Sopha DEBRIS | 61 | F | Mulatto | |
| Catherine | 26 | F | Mulatto | |
| Sally | 6 | F | Mulatto | |
| Charles | 3 | M | Mulatto | |
| Fanny D. | 10 mos. | F | Mulatto | |
| 63. Henry DEBRISS | 35 | M | Mulatto | Shoemaker |
| Catherine | 35 | F | Black | Washerwoman |
| Catherine Jr. | 16 | F | Mulatto | House Servant |
| Ned | 12 | M | Mulatto | House Servant |
| Hellen | 8 | F | Mulatto | House Servant |
| Bettie | 7 | F | Mulatto | House Servant |
| Polly | 5 | F | Mulatto | |
| Howard Debris | 19 | M | Mulatto | Field Servant |
| 64. Bettie SHEPERD | 55 | F | Black | Washerwoman |
| Rebecca JONES | 60 | F | Black | Washerwoman |
| Julia | 26 | F | Black | Washerwoman |
| Willimes(?) | 5 | M | Mulatto | |

| #. Name | Age | Sex | Race | Occupation |
|---|---|---|---|---|
| 65. _____ | | | | |
| 66. Jane PAGE | 25 | F | Black | Washerwoman |
| Wm. | 2 | M | Black | |
| 67. Morning COLEMAN | 50 | F | Black | Washerwoman |
| 68. Robt. J. GRIFFIN | 28 | M | | Waterman |
| Mary A. | 22 | F | | Seamstress |
| Jane E. | 1 | F | | |
| 69. Catharine BROWN | 75 | F | Mulatto | |
| Henry COOK | 80 | M | Black | Gardener |
| 70. Joseph WALTHALL | 30 | M | | Shoemaker |
| Susan | 32 | F | | |
| Richd. HUBBARD | 69 | M | | Shoemaker |
| Thos. A Walthall | 8 | M | | |
| 71. Isaac HOFHEIMER | 43 | M | | Merchant |
| Regina | 45 | F | | |
| Allex | 14 | M | | |
| Caroline | 12 | F | | |
| David | 8 | M | | |
| Zack | 6 | M | | |
| Isadore(?) | 4 | M | | |
| Christopher JAMES | 12 | M | Black | |
| 72. Wm H. LEE(R?) | 64 | M | | Merchant |
| Susan | 54 | F | | |
| Wm. H. Jr. | 20 | M | | Mechanic |
| Edward I.(?) M. | 16 | M | | |

| #. Name | Age | Sex | Race | Occupation |
|---|---|---|---|---|
| 73. Jno. H. BARLOW | 52 | M | | Merchant |
| M.M. | 52 | F | | |
| Jno. H. Jr. | 21 | M | | Merchant |
| Thos I. | 18 | M | | |
| Emma C. | 15 | F | | |
| Louisa | 13 | F | | |
| 74. James(?) HELLER(?) | 39 | M | | Merchant/Agent |
| Polina(?) | 28 | F | | |
| Charles | 11 | M | | |
| Catherine | 7 | F | | |
| Ida | 4 | F | | |
| Geo. W.E. | 4 mos. | M | | |
| 75. Leonard HENLEY | 39 | M | | Physician |
| Rebecca | 29 | F | | |
| Elizabeth R. | 3 | F | | |
| 76. John S. DIX | 53 | M | | Merchant |
| Sally H. | 53 | F | | |
| Henry S. | 16 | M | | |
| John G. | 14 | M | | |
| ___ A. SCARBURGH | 54 | F | | |
| James H. Dix | 16 | M | | |
| Sally E. | 22 | F | | |
| 77. Felix LOGUE(?) | 31 | M | | Shoemaker |
| 78. Peter T.(?) POWELL | 37 | M | | Merchant |
| Louisiana | 35 | F | | |
| Jno. __ SIMCOE | 22 | M | | Store Clerk |
| Susan C. Powell | 11 | F | | |

| #. Name | Age | Sex | Race | Occupation |
|---|---|---|---|---|
| Anna P. | 9 | F | | |
| Philip E. | 7 | M | | |
| Cassie | 4 | F | | |
| F.U. | 2 | M | | |
| Cecilia | 1 | F | | |
| 79. Richd. GRAVES | 45 | M | | Sadler & Harness Maker |
| Elizabeth M. | 42 | F | | |
| _____ | 15 | F | | |
| Henry K. | 12 | M | | |
| Wm. P. | 10 | M | | |
| Charles B. | 3 | M | | |
| Charles B. C____LAY | 27 | M | | Harness Maker |
| 80. Dr. S.S. GRIFFIN | 79 | M | | Physician |
| Mary L. WRIGHT | 42 | F | | |
| Sally L. | 21 | F | | |
| Nancy BROWN | 21 | F | | |
| 81. Nicholas BURRIDGE | 50 | M | | Mechanic |
| Maria | 44 | F | | |
| Maria Jr. | 10 | F | | |
| Charles W. | 7 | M | | |
| 82. Walter CUMBER | 30 | M | Mulatto | Fireman on Steamboat |
| Mary I.(?) | 30 | F | Black | Washerwoman |
| Lucy A. | 3 | F | Mulatto | |
| 83. Wm. L. VAUGHAN | 32 | M | | Mechanic |
| Isabella | 19 | F | | |

| #. Name | Age | Sex | Race | Occupation |
|---|---|---|---|---|
| Jno. H. | 11 | M | | |
| Sarah F. | 1 | F | | |
| 84. Henry PETERS | 33 | M | | Grocer |
| Elizabeth | 29 | F | | |
| Wm. H. | 7 | M | | |
| Isabella | 6 | F | | |
| 85. M. HOFHEIMER | 36 | M | | Merchant |
| Jennie | 33 | F | | |
| Henry | 11 | M | | |
| Mollie | 9 | F | | |
| Eliza | 7 | F | | |
| Henrietta | 3 | F | | |
| Alex | 3 mos. | | | |
| 86. Charlotte MORRISON | 72 | F | | |
| Emilie | 37 | F | | |
| Jno. H. | 35 | M | | Store Clerk |
| Fred P. | 17 | M | | Store Clerk |
| 87. Henry V. MORRIS | 44 | M | | Police Officer |
| Mary E. | 30 | F | | |
| Elmira | 16 | F | | |
| Sally W. | 14 | F | | |
| Caroline C. | 10 | F | | |
| Octavious T. | 1 | M | | |
| Bettie F. | 2 mos. | F | | |
| Milly FORDEN | 13 | F | | House Servant |
| Allen LINDSAY | 38 | M | | Mechanic |

| #. Name | Age | Sex | Race | Occupation |
|---|---|---|---|---|
| 88. Mary HALL | 50 | F | Mulatto | Washerwoman |
| Eli CARTER | 8 | M | Black | |
| Wm. Carter | 6 | M | Mulatto | |
| Susan A. Carter | 3 | F | Mulatto | |
| John Hall | 23 | M | Black | Servant |
| 89. Rhoda WRIGHT | 60 | F | Mulatto | House Servant |
| 90. William COLEMAN | 57 | M | Black | Ditcher |
| Mary | 54 | F | Black | Seamstress |
| 91. Henry COLEMAN | 30 | M | Black | Ditcher |
| Kitty | 22 | F | Black | Washerwoman |
| Mary I. | 3 | F | Black | |
| 92. John ASHBY | 36 | M | Black | Waterman |
| Jane | 35 | F | Mulatto | Washerwoman |
| Sally GARY | 10 | F | Mulatto | |
| Mat ASHBY | 4 | M | Mulatto | |
| Mary A. Ashby | 1 | F | Mulatto | |
| 93. Mary TALIAFERRO | 50 | F | Mulatto | Washerwoman |
| Jno. R. | 20 | M | Black | Oysterman |
| Elizabeth | 18 | F | Mulatto | Washerwoman |
| George H. | 16 | M | Mulatto | |
| Peter I. | 14 | M | Black | |
| Anna | 12 | F | Mulatto | |
| 94. Robt. JACKSON | 30 | M | Black | Ditcher |
| Julia | 25 | F | Black | Washerwoman |
| Wm. Jackson | 3 | M | Black | |
| Octavia | 6 | F | Black | |

| #. Name | Age | Sex | Race | Occupation |
|---|---|---|---|---|
| 95. Pryor MERCER | 24 | M | Mulatto | Woodcutter |
| 96. Isaac GREEN | 48 | M | Black | Woodcutter |
| Mary | 30 | F | Black | Washerwoman |
| Jas. H. | 8 | M | Black | |
| 97. Frances MERCER | 30 | F | Mulatto | Washerwoman |
| Wm. DODD | 6 | M | Mulatto | |
| Jas. COLEMAN | 21 | M | Mulatto | |
| 98. Chas C.P. WALLER | 38 | M | Farmer | |
| Nannie C. | 30 | F | | |
| Jno. B. | 10 | M | | |
| Agnes T. | 2 | F | | |
| Mary A. LASKE | 60 | F | | |
| 99. Roctilda ROLLERSON | 46 | F | Mulatto | Washerwoman |
| 100. Lucy A. TUCKER | 47 | F | | |
| Cynthia B.T. WASHINGTON | 27 | F | | |
| St. Geo. B. Tucker | 21 | M | | Physician |
| Thomas S. B. | 18 | M | | |
| Fannie B. | 16 | F | | |
| Henrietta B. | 14 | F | | |
| B.M.B. | 12 | M | | |
| Sarah J. Washington | 3 | F | | |
| 101. P.M. THOMPSON | 43 | M | | Lawyer |
| Julia | 41 | F | | |

| #. Name | Age | Sex | Race | Occupation |
|---|---|---|---|---|
| 102. Wm. PEACHY | 41 | M | | Lawyer |
| Virginia B. | 39 | F | | |
| Wm. D. | 15 | M | | |
| Eliza K. | 14 | F | | |
| Maria D. | 9 | F | | |
| Sally C. | 7 | F | | |
| Thos. G. | 4 | M | | |
| Bathurst | 2 | M | | |
| Archer C. | 3 mos. | M | | |
| Charity | 9 | F | Black | House Servant |
| 103. R.R. ROPER | 34 | M | | Mechanic |
| Frances P. | 28 | F | | |
| Wm. O. | 2 | M | | |
| Mary L. YERBY | 2 | F | | |
| 104. John F. DAUGHERTY | 41 | M | | Waterman |
| Lucy J. | 24 | F | | |
| Jno. Jr. | 4 | M | | |
| Mary W. | 2 | F | | |
| Richard B. | 8 mos. | M | | |
| Eliza BAKER | 13 | F | Black | House Servant |
| 105. Jas. L. HENDERSON | 45 | M | | Capt. U.S.N. |
| Sarah L. | 36 | F | | |
| Thos. W. | 15 | M | | |
| 106. R. McCANDLISH | 44 | F | | |
| Thos. P. | 23 | M | | |
| H.S. | 20 | M | | |
| Robert | 16 | M | | |
| Mary M. | 8 | F | | |

| #. Name | Age | Sex | Race | Occupation |
|---------|-----|-----|------|------------|
| 107. Thos. MOSS | 52 | M | | Coachmaker |
| Wm. E. | 28 | M | | Coachmaker |
| Geo. E. | 18 | M | | Coachmaker |
| Chas. H. HARPER | 29 | M | | Coachmaker |
| 108. Julia WARBURTON | 38 | F | | Mantuamaker |
| Mary C. | 28 | F | | Mantuamaker |
| 109. Gabriella WILLIAMSON | 35 | F | | |
| James WOOLFOLK | 27 | M | | Teacher |
| Jno. A.G. Williamson | 15 | M | | |
| Chas. P. | 12 | M | | |
| Mary Gay Williamson | 9 | F | | |
| 110. Arrena PLEASANTS | 50 | F | Black | Washerwoman |
| John | 10 | M | Black | House Servant |
| Grace | 5 | F | Black | |
| 111. R.M. BUCKTROUT | 54 | M | | Undertaker |
| Celes(?) | 21 | F | | |
| Delia | 14 | F | | |
| 112. William CORRAW(?) | 50 | M | | Brickmason |
| 113. Dr. Jno. M. GALT | 41 | M | | Physician |
| Miss Sallie M. Galt | 38 | F | | |
| Lucy JONES | 60 | F | Black | Washerwoman |
| 114. Sarah MOUNTFORTH | 54 | F | | |
| Martha BINGLEY | 80 | F | | |
| 115. Christopher WHITING | 67 | M | | Coachmaker |
| Thos. H. Whiting | 34 | M | | Painter |

| #. Name | Age | Sex | Race | Occupation |
|---|---|---|---|---|
| Mary E. | 22 | F | | |
| Martha A. WILSON | 40 | F | | |
| Emily R. Whiting | 3 | F | | |
| Thomas S. | 2 mos. | M | | |
| 116. Peter I. CLOWES | 54 | M | | Farmer |
| Sarah I. | 46 | F | | |
| Texas B. | 15 | M | | |
| John H. MEARS | 7 | M | | |
| Sarah J.F KELLIAM | 39 | F | | |
| 117. S.W. BLAIN | 52 | M | | Minister |
| Susan J. | 52 | F | | |
| Daniel | 21 | M | | Teacher |
| Mary R. | 19 | F | | |
| R.W. | 17 | M | | |
| Charlotte E. | 14 | F | | |
| Lucy C. | 11 | F | | |
| 118. Robt. BLASSINGHAM | 49 | M | | Merchant |
| Eudoxie(?) | 15 | F | | |
| John | 13 | M | | |
| Meso (?) | 9 | F | | |
| John COX | 38 | M | | Brick Mason |
| 119. John POTTS | 28 | M | | Mechanic |
| Helen | 21 | H | | |
| 120. Wm. LINDSAY | 27 | M | | Mechanic |
| Sarah H. | 21 | F | | |
| Wm. E. | 3 mos. | M | | |

| #. Name | Age | Sex | Race | Occupation |
|---|---|---|---|---|
| 121. Isaac SMITH | 44 | M | | Merchant |
| Susan A.V. | 31 | F | | |
| Charles | 16 | M | | |
| Isaac | 12 | M | | |
| George T. | 9 | M | | |
| Elizabeth | 7 | F | | |
| Elizabeth PARSONS | 17 | F | Black | Servant |
| Mary A. BOLTON | 76 | F | | Seamstress |
| 122. John SLAUGHTER | 66 | M | | |
| Mildred | 50 | F | | |
| Levenia LAWSON | 22 | F | | |
| John W. Lawson | 21 | M | | |
| Evie(?) A. HUGHS | 45 | F | | |
| 123. John C. LUCAS | 37 | M | | Mechanic |
| Ann C. | 36 | F | | |
| Sarah J. | 64 | F | | |
| John C. Jr. | 11 | M | | |
| James T. | 9 | M | | |
| Mary E. | 4 | M | | |
| Sarah | 1 | F | | |
| 124. James H. MAHONE | 26 | M | | Blacksmith |
| Elizabeth | 21 | F | | |
| Chas. L. | 3 | M | | |
| Lotey(?) SMITH | 50 | F | Black | Washerwoman |
| 125. Wm. J TALIAFERRO | 23 | M | Black | Wheelwright |
| Mary M. | 18 | F | Mulatto | Washerwoman |

| #. Name | Age | Sex | Race | Occupation |
|---|---|---|---|---|
| 126. James M. MAHONE | 53 | M | | Farmer |
| Sarah M. | 58 | F | | |
| Thos. B. | 12 | M | | |
| Thos. M. WARE | 4 | M | | |
| 127. Chas. LIVELY | 58 | M | | Waterman |
| Jane E. | 49 | F | | |
| Imogene | 14 | F | | |
| Sarah F. | 12 | F | | |
| Jane STEPHENSON | 10 | F | | |
| Sarah BUTT | 35 | F | | |
| Dallas JONES | 17 | M | Black | Waterman |
| Thadeous GILLIAM | 21 | M | | Waterman |
| 128. Martha MURDOUGH | 27 | F | Mulatto | Seamstress |
| Christianna | 9 | F | Mulatto | |
| Elizabeth | 6 | F | Mulatto | |
| 129. Sarah BURKES | 29 | F | Black | Seamstress |
| Emma Jane | 10 | F | Black | |
| 130. Cornelias JOHNSON | 34 | M | | |
| Mary Johnson | 37 | F | | |
| Maria BOWERS | 35 | F | | |
| Julia A Johnson | 11 | F | | |
| Sarah E. | 9 | F | | |
| Rosa B. | 6 | F | | |
| John H. Bowers | 5 | M | | |
| 131. Robert J. BARLOW | 45 | M | | Mechanic |
| Louisa A. | 46 | F | | Milliner |

| #. Name | Age | Sex | Race | Occupation |
|---|---|---|---|---|
| Willie R. | 8 | M | | |
| Godfrey ANNFIELD | 30 | M | Mulatto | Farmhand |
| 132. Islie(?) BARRETT | 50 | F | Mulatto | Washerwoman |
| 133. Josiah THOMAS | 34 | M | | Mail Carrier |
| Margarett E. | 27 | F | | Dress Maker |
| Laura A. | 8 | F | | |
| Josephine M. | 6 | F | | |
| John N. | 4 | M | | |
| Mary | 1 | F | | |
| 134. Joanna THOMAS | 58 | F | | Seamstress |
| Sarah PUGH | 56 | F | | |
| 135. Col. G. DURFEY | 59 | M | Farmer | |
| Margarett W. | 45 | F | | |
| Elizabeth HORRICUTT | 25 | F | | |
| Margarett Durfey | 15 | F | | |
| Zackry G. | 11 | M | | |
| Elizabeth | 9 | F | | |
| 136. Alex POWELL | 36 | M | | Farmer |
| Elizabeth J. | 34 | F | | |
| Peter Jr. | 13 | M | | |
| Alexander Jr. | 12 | M | | |
| Sarah E. | 9 | F | | |
| Wm. H. | 7 | M | | |
| Harriett A. | 5 | F | | |
| Jas. B. | 3 | M | | |
| Judson C. | 1 | M | | |

| #. Name | Age | Sex | Race | Occupation |
|---------|-----|-----|------|------------|
| 137. Alexander LAWSON | 30 | M | | Mechanic |
| Sarah J. | 21 | F | | |
| Ella L. | 4 | F | | |
| Charles | 1 | M | | |
| 138. James M. JOHNSON | 29 | M | | Merchant |
| Mary A. | 25 | F | | |
| Louisa D. | 6 | F | | |
| Mary E. | 4 | F | | |
| John Wm. | 8 mos. | M | | |
| 139. Charlotte U_____ | 28 | F | Mulatto | Seamstress |
| 140. Mrs. Mary H. CLAIBURN | 50 | F | | |
| 141. Wm. W. VEST | 51 | M | | Merchant |
| Eliza A. | 51 | F | | |
| Eliza W. JOYNES | 25 | F | | |
| Edward S. Joynes | 26 | M | | Professor of G&L |
| Walker W. Vest | 24 | M | | Lawyer |
| Pattie G. Vest | 20 | F | | |
| George S. Vest | 14 | M | | |
| Willie W. Vest | 11 | F | | |
| 142. William WILBURN | 48 | M | | Waterman |
| Catharine | 28 | F | | |
| 143. George W. JACKSON | 59 | M | | Mechanic |
| Lovett S. | 45 | F | | Mantua Maker |
| Martha WHITING | 37 | F | | Mantua Maker |
| George W. Jackson Jr. | 18 | M | | Painter |
| Louisa MAHONE | 15 | F | | |

| #. Name | Age | Sex | Race | Occupation |
|---|---|---|---|---|
| 144. Dr. R.P. WALLER | 67 | M | | Farmer |
| Mrs. J.W. Waller | 55 | F | | |
| H.M. Waller | 30 | M | | |
| J.W. Waller | 21 | F | | |
| C.J. Waller | 20 | F | | |
| 145. Dr. Rob. M. GARRETT | 51 | M | | Physician |
| Susan C. | 45 | F | | |
| Wm. R. | 21 | M | | Lawyer |
| H. Winder Garrett | 15 | M | | |
| Van T. | 13 | M | | |
| Charlotte G. | 11 | F | | |
| Mary L. | 9 | F | | |
| Susan W. | 7 | F | | |
| Lauretta SAVAGE | 51 | F | | |
| 146. Gabriella GALT | 40 | F | | |
| 147. Andrew LYTLE | 41 | M | | Manufacturer |
| Joanna P. | 36 | F | | |
| Henry B. | 10 | M | | |
| Alice M. | 8 | F | | |
| Felton M. | 7 mos. | M | | |
| 148. Thos. A. MOSS | 27 | M | | Coachmaker |
| Suzy F. | 25 | F | | |
| Allen A. | 5 | M | | |
| William F. | 4 | M | | |
| Henry G. | 1 | M | | |
| Ed. P. | 6 mos. | M | | |
| Alphonso MOORLAND(?) | 24 | M | | Carpenter |

| #. Name | Age | Sex | Race | Occupation |
|---|---|---|---|---|
| E.T. CLEMANS | age(?) | M | | |
| Elizabeth Clemans | age(?) | F | | |
| 149. Benj. T. MARNER | 30 | M | | Mechanic |
| Sarah | 18 | F | | |
| Cora | 1 | F | | |
| Wm. BAILEY | 17 | M | | |
| 150. Charlotte DAVIS | 50 | F | | |
| 151. Charles C. HANSFORD | 35 | M | | Clerk |
| 152. John Y. JESTER | 28 | M | | Mechanic |
| Celina | 20 | F | | |
| Ann E. SMITH | 16 | F | | |
| Jas. H Jester | 1 | M | | |
| 153. S.T. BOWMAN | 45 | M | | Farmer |
| Elizabeth | 46 | F | | |
| Joseph | 35 | M | | Mechanic |
| 154. H.M. LEE | 53 | M | | Officer at E.L. Asylum |
| Ann E. Lee | 53 | F | | |
| Wm. H. Lee | 21 | M | | Mechanic |
| Peyton Ann BURNETTE | 16 | F | | |
| Candis(?) | 19 | F | Mulatto | Servant |
| 155. J.H. HOPE | 41 | M | | Hotel Keeper |
| Cornelia | 20 | F | | |
| Rosilia | 14 | F | | |
| Lucious EDLOE | 37 | M | | |

| #. Name | Age | Sex | Race | Occupation |
|---|---|---|---|---|
| 156. Wm. M. YOUNG | 33 | M | | Minister (Baptist) |
| C.P. | 30 | F | | |
| Judy BRIGGS | 40 | F | Mulatto | House Servant |
| 157. John H. HENLEY | 42 | M | | Clerk of Circuit Court |
| H.T. Henley | 60 | F | | |
| Lucy A. CARY | 35 | F | | |
| Harriett Cary | 21 | F | | |
| W. Miles Cary | 16 | M | | |
| Mattie PIERCE | 21 | F | | |
| 158. Richd. GILLIAM | 56 | M | | |
| Elizabeth E. | 56 | F | | |
| Roberta | 18 | F | | |
| Benja. | 16 | M | | |
| 159. Henry M. BOWDEN | 43 | M | | Farmer |
| Henryetta | 39 | F | | |
| Eudora J. STUBBLEFIELD | 19 | F | | |
| Alice D. Bowden | 15 | F | | |
| Geo. E. | 7 | M | | |
| Susan MAYER | 47 | F | | |
| 160. Leroy CASEY | 53 | M | | Shoemaker |
| Mary A. | 55 | F | | Seamstress |
| Henrietta MAHONE | 15 | F | | Seamstress |
| 161. Jas. T.H. WALKINS | 28 | M | | Agent for soap |
| 162. Moses R. HOWEL | 53 | M | | Farmer |
| M.R. Howel Jr. | 17 | M | | |

| #. Name | Age | Sex | Race | Occupation |
|---|---|---|---|---|
| Julia M. | 13 | F | | |
| Thomas J. | 11 | M | | |
| Isaac CUSTIS | 40 | M | Black | House Servant |
| 163. Wm. G. LUMPKIN | 26 | M | | Meth. Minister |
| 164. Wm TAYLOR | 25 | M | | Farm Laborer |
| Eliza A. | 23 | F | | Seamstress |
| Sarah A. | 2 | F | | |
| 165. Robert H. ARMISTEAD | 56 | M | | Lawyer |
| Julia S. | 39 | F | | |
| Rob. F. | 15 | M | | |
| Wm. C. | 11 | M | | |
| Harry T. | 7 | M | | |
| Cary P. | 3 | M | | |
| Julia M. | 1 | F | | |
| Maria F. PEYTON | 60 | F | | |
| Wm. J.(?) DODD | 19 | M | | Field Laborer |
| Eliza BARKER | 21 | F | | Seamstress |
| 166. Jno. E. PIERCE | 47 | M | | Mechanic |
| Nerick(?) ENNIS | 30 | M | Mulatto | Laborer |
| 167. Jas. W. CUSTIS | 49 | M | | Farmer |
| Clara H. | 45 | F | | |
| Leah JAYMES | 61 | F | | |
| C.W. Custis | 18 | F | | |
| M.T. | 16 | F | | |
| E.F. | 15 | F | | |
| Florence | 10 | F | | |

| #. Name | Age | Sex | Race | Occupation |
|---|---|---|---|---|
| 168. Julia TAYLOR | 55 | F | | |
| Emma PENDLETON | 24 | F | | |
| Leonard Taylor | 18 | M | | |
| Nannie | 13 | F | | |
| Claudia Pendleton | 3 | F | | |
| Wm. Pendleton | 2 | M | | |
| 169. Lucy W. BRYAN | 71 | F | | |
| 170. Wm. H. PIERCE | 52 | M | | Commissioner Of Revenue |
| Rebecca | 42 | F | | |
| John W. | 20 | M | | Prescriptionist |
| Wm. H. Pierce Jr. | 18 | M | | |
| 171. Rosco LIPSCOMB | 56 | M | | |
| Jane M. | 49 | F | | |
| Mary J. | 28 | F | | |
| Spotswood | 20 | M | | |
| Rosco | 18 | M | | |
| Cornelia | 16 | F | | |
| Emma | 12 | F | | |
| Anna | 10 | F | | |
| Frank | 8 | M | | |
| Claiborne | 3 | M | | |
| 172. Samuel F. BRIGHT | 56 | M | | Farmer |
| Elizabeth B. | 48 | F | | |
| S.E. EDLOE | 26 | F | | |
| Robert A. Bright | 21 | M | | |
| Jean St. C. Bright | 9 | F | | |

| #. Name | Age | Sex | Race | Occupation |
|---|---|---|---|---|
| 173. Richd. W. HANSFORD | 39 | M | | Merchant |
| Sarah | 72 | F | | |
| M.B. WELLS | 48 | F | | |
| S.H. Hansford | 42 | F | | |
| S.W. | 37 | F | | |
| Rebecca | 35 | F | | |
| Martha WORTON | 44 | F | | |
| Eliza Worton | 42 | F | | |
| Richd. C. WHITAKER | 21 | M | | Store Clerk |
| 174. Wm. M. GOODMAN | 47 | M | | Ward Officer E.L. Asylum |
| Virginia A. | 37 | F | | |
| Angelina C. | 16 | F | | |
| Sally B. | 13 | F | | |
| Julia | 5 | F | | |
| 175. Jaceman(?) BADKINS | 25 | F | | |
| Wm. Badkins | 9 | M | | |
| Fanny | 7 | F | | |
| Ann | 5 | F | | |
| Emma | 2 | F | | |
| Martha | 14 | F | | |
| 176. Col. D. PRYOR | 60 | M | | School Teacher |
| B. | 35 | F | | |
| M.E. | 7 | F | | |
| S.T. | 5 | F | | |
| Wm. A. | 3 | M | | |
| Geo. W. | 1 | M | | |

| #. Name | Age | Sex | Race | Occupation |
|---|---|---|---|---|
| 177. Geo. W. HORNSBY | 34 | M | | Plasterer |
| Mary C. | 33 | F | | |
| E.A. | 4 | F | | |
| Georgiana | 1 | F | | |
| 178. Jno. C. MERCER | 49 | M | | Physician |
| Mary C. | 40 | F | | |
| Mary L. | 21 | F | | |
| Eliza C. | 19 | F | | |
| Thos. H. | 16 | M | | |
| Corben W. | 14 | M | | |
| Catherine S. | 12 | F | | |
| John S. | 10 | M | | |
| Robt. P. | 8 | M | | |
| Isabella S. | 4 | F | | |
| Geo. W. | 2 | M | | |
| 179. Parke SLATER | 44 | M | | Sergeant |
| Virginia | 35 | F | | |
| — | field age(?) | M | | |
| James | 13 | M | | |
| Virginia Slater | 12 | F | | |
| Calhoun | 7 | M | | |
| Cordelia | 3 | F | | |
| May | 1 | F | | |
| 180. Sarah SAUNDERS | 40 | F | | |
| Mary | 46 | F | | |

| #. Name | Age | Sex | Race | Occupation |
|---|---|---|---|---|
| 181. Mary H. BOWERS | 75 | F | | |
| Eliza | 40 | F | | |
| 182. Parkey Jeno(?) CLARK | 30 | F | | Tayloress |
| Mattie | 14 | F | | |
| Philmes(?) | 12 | M | | |
| Wm. C. Clark | 10 | M | | |
| Mary | 6 | F | | |
| John | 21 | M | | Mechanic |
| 183. Richd. BOWRY | 35 | M | | Ward Officer of E.L. Asylum |
| Mary A. | 25 | F | | |
| Ella | 9 | F | | |
| Walter | 6 | M | | |
| Mary | 5 | F | | |
| Richd. | 2 | M | | |
| Maria T. BASSETT | 16 | F | | |
| Catharine | 19 | F | Black | House Servant |
| Lucy JAMES | 30 | F | Black | Washerwoman |
| 184. Rob. A BOERY | 21 | M | | Mechanic |
| Bushrod | 16 | M | | |
| 185. Robt. P. TAYLOR | 28 | M | | Steward for E.L. Asylum |
| Sally H. | 26 | F | | |
| R.W. | 4 mos. | M | | |
| Mary A. Taylor | 43 | F | | |

| #. Name | Age | Sex | Race | Occupation |
|---------|-----|-----|------|------------|
| 186. Susan M. CHRISTIAN | 46 | F | | Matron of E.L. Asylum |
| WM. T. Christian | 24 | M | | "D. M. E. D. Va." |
| E.A. Christian | 20 | F | | |
| E.P. | 18 | F | | |
| Sue W. GALT | 6 | F | | |
| 187. Jno. K. NOEL | 43 | M | | School Teacher |
| Mary LEWIS | 84 | F | | |
| Lydia DONNE | 40 | F | | Teacher |
| 188. Samuel W. HEATLY(?) | 50 | M | | Music Professor |
| Louisa | 30 | F | | |
| Maria Jr. | 6 | F | | |
| Jane | 4 | F | | |
| Lilly | 2 | F | | |
| 189. Susan BROWN | 50 | F | Black | Washerwoman |
| 190. George GRIMES | 60 | M | Black | Oysterman |
| Betsy | 40 | F | Mulatto | Seamstress |
| James | 14 | M | Mulatto | |
| Billy | 11 | M | Mulatto | |
| Isakiah(?) | 5 | F | Mulatto | |
| 191. Mrs. S.M. ALLEN | 45 | F | | School Teacher |
| 192. David(?) SMITH | 61 | M | Black | Farm Laborer |
| 193. J.F. BOWEN | 28 | M | | Suprnt. Of Gal(?) |

| #. Name | Age | Sex | Race | Occupation |
|---|---|---|---|---|
| 194. Jno. A. Thompson | 46 | M | | Ward Officer of E.L. Asylum |
| Wm. CONLEY | 40 | M | | Ward Officer of E.L. Asylum |
| 195. Mrs. M. BOWRY | 50 | F | | Ward Officer of E.L. Asylum |
| E.C. WARE | 56 | F | | |
| Mrs. S. ROPER | 50 | F | | |
| Mrs. Caroline(?) LINDSAY | 45 | F | | |
| E.S. Ware | 60 | F | | |
| 196. Dr. M. WILLIAMSON | 54 | M | | Physician |
| Mary K. Williamson | 46 | F | | |
| Miss Rosa DIXON | 33 | F | | |
| Bette Dixon | 14 | F | | |
| Samuel | 11 | M | | |
| 197. Richd. BARKER | 24 | M | | Common Laborer |
| 198. Edward CAMM Sr. | 53 | M | | Physician |
| Mrs. E. Camm | 41 | F | | |
| T.W. | 24 | M | | Clerk at E.L. Asylum |
| Edward Jr. | 21 | M | | |
| Charlie | 15 | M | | |
| Frank | 12 | M | | |
| Govan(?) | 8 | M | | |
| Florence | 4 | F | | |
| John | 3 | M | | |
| Infant not named | 11 mos. | F | | |

| #. Name | Age | Sex | Race | Occupation |
|---|---|---|---|---|
| 199. J.B. COSENHAN | 35 | M | | Lawyer |
| Ellen | 25 | F | | |
| Roberta | 16 | F | | |
| Robert W. | 13 | M | | |
| Mary | 10 | F | | |
| Carlin(?) | 8 | M | | |
| Hugh M. | 6 | M | | |
| Louisa | 1 | F | | |
| 200. Mrs. ANDERSON | 77 | F | | |
| Matilda SOUTHALL | 50 | F | | |

Appendix B

# THE WILLIAMSBURG JUNIOR GUARD

Under the antebellum Virginia militia system, which was based on the Federal Militia Act of 1792, all free white males between the ages of eighteen and forty-five were liable for military duty if needed by the governor. Minus certain exemptions (such as state and local officials, millers, ferrymen, firemen, police, school commissioners and trustees, etc.), all persons subject to military call-up were required to be enrolled in their local militia company or regiment.

Officially, the militia unit of James City and York Counties, which included the city of Williamsburg area, was the Sixty-Eighth Regiment of the Ninth Brigade, Virginia Militia. In addition to the "line" militia, however, certain "volunteer" battalions were authorized by the Virginia Assembly in 1851 and 1852. These volunteers were uniformed at their own expense and held their own drills and meetings.

After John Brown's raid on Harper's Ferry in October 1859, such a volunteer company was formed by concerned local citizens. Named the "Williamsburg Junior Guard," it conducted training and drills throughout 1860 and proudly participated in several parades.

With the secession crisis of early 1861, students of the College of William & Mary attempted to form a "college" company uniformed in red flannel shirts and jean cloth trousers. Their proposed weaponry were bowie knives and double-barreled shotguns. The college faculty went as far as requesting two brass cannons from the governor in order to drill the students.

When Virginia formally seceded in late April 1861, the college company disbanded as the students returned to distant homes to join their local units. The Williamsburg Junior Guard combined with the remnants of the college company and was mustered into state service under the command of the president of the College of William & Mary, Benjamin Ewell, who was commissioned as a major in the Army of the State of Virginia. As Virginia joined the new Confederate States in June, the Junior Guard became Company C, Thirty-Second Virginia Infantry, and served throughout the war.

The original roster of the Williamsburg Junior Guard from April 1861 listed the following men as members of the company:

CAPTAIN: J.A. Henley

FIRST LIEUTENANT: William Morecock

SECOND LIEUTENANT: H.M. Waller

THIRD LIEUTENANT: L. Henley

ORDERLY SERGEANT: O.N. Coke

SECOND SERGEANT: P. Jones

THIRD SERGEANT: J.F. Bowry

FOURTH SERGEANT: R.L. Henley

FIFTH SERGEANT: W.T. Christian

COLOR-BEARER: W.E. Moss

FIRST CORPORAL: A.I. Hofheimer

SECOND CORPORAL: R.A. Bowry

THIRD CORPORAL: W.W. Lee

FOURTH CORPORAL: W.H. Barlow

PRIVATES: J.H. Barlow Jr., T.J. Barlow, R.G. Barlow, G.O. Ball, J.V. Bidgood, William Burke, R. Barham, W. Miles Cary, J.W. Clarke, C.B. Coakley, R. Crandall, T.C. Carrington, G.W. Clowes, J.A. Davis, J.W. Davis, S.N. Deneufville, H.L. Dix, J.H. Dix, W.C. Durfey, W.F. Gilliam, W.G. Gatewood, Benjamin Gilliam, R.J. Griffin, J.R. Harwood, J.M. Johnson, G.W. Jackson, H.T. Jones Jr., J.C. Lucus, W.H. Lee, E.M. Lee, R.A. Lively, E.H. Lively, R.C. Lawson, L. Lukehard, A.J. Lane, T.A. Moss, J.A.J. Moss, G.H. Mercer, H.V. Morris, H.A. Morris, J.W. Morris, F.P. Morrison, S. Maupin, C.W. Mahone, D.R. Mahone, J.H. Mahone, H.L. McCandlish, H.P. Moore, R. Owens, B.F. Piggott, J.T. Parham, B.H. Radcliffe, J. Radcliffe, C.H. Richardson, L.P. Slater, J. Simcoe, S. Simcoe, M. Spraggins, R.B. Shelburne, I. Smith, Talbot Sweeney, F.R. Sykes, L. Taylor, R.P. Taylor, William Vaughn, T.H. Whiting, J.T.H. Wilkins, J.B. Wilkins, William Wilkins, A.L. Williamson, J.M. Walthall, W.H. Yerby

MARKERS: B.W. Bowry, J.M. Maupin

Of this 1861 roster, many are known to have had various degrees of service in this and other units throughout the war. Only four men from the original Williamsburg Junior Guard surrendered at Appomattox in April 1865.

Appendix C

# THE ARMIES OF THE
# BATTLE OF WILLIAMSBURG

## *May 5, 1862*

**Confederate**

Army Commander: General Joseph E. Johnston

Field Commander: Major General James Longstreet

Second Division: Major General James Longstreet

Hill's Brigade: Brigadier General Ambrose Powell Hill
First Virginia
Seventh Virginia
Eleventh Virginia
Seventeenth Virginia

Anderson's Brigade: Brigadier General Richard H. Anderson
Fourth South Carolina Battalion
Fifth South Carolina
Sixth South Carolina
Palmetto Sharpshooters
Louisiana Foot Rifles
Fauquier Artillery
Williamsburg Artillery
Richmond Howitzers

Pickett's Brigade: Brigadier General George E. Pickett
Eighth Virginia
Eighteenth Virginia
Nineteenth Virginia
Twenty-Eighth Virginia
Dearing's Virginia Battery

Wilcox's Brigade: Brigadier General Cadmus M. Wilcox
Ninth Alabama
Tenth Alabama
Nineteenth Mississippi

Pryor's Brigade: Brigadier General Roger A. Pryor
Eighth Alabama
Fourteenth Alabama
Fourteenth Louisiana
Thirty-Second Virginia (detachment)
Richmond Fayette Artillery

Colston's Brigade: Brigadier General Raleigh E. Colston
Third Virginia
Thirteenth North Carolina
Fourteenth North Carolina
Donaldsonville Louisiana Battery

Forth Division: Major General Daniel H. Hill

Early's Brigade: Brigadier General Jubal A. Early
Twenty-Fourth Virginia
Thirty-Eighth Virginia
Fifth North Carolina
Twenty-Third North Carolina

Rhodes Brigade: Brigadier General Robert E. Rodes
Second Florida
Second Mississippi Battalion

Cavalry Division: Brigadier General James E. B. Stuart
First Virginia Cavalry
Third Virginia Cavalry
Fourth Virginia Cavalry
Wise's Legion
Jeff Davis Legion
Stuart Horse Artillery

## Union

Army Commander: Major General George B. McClellan

Field Commander: Brigadier General Edwin V. Sumner

III Corps: Brigadier General Samuel P. Heintzelman

Second Division: Brigadier General Joseph Hooker

First Brigade: Brigadier General Cuvier Grover
First Massachusetts
Eleventh Massachusetts
Second New Hampshire
Twenty-Sixth Pennsylvania

Second Brigade: Colonel Nelson Taylor
Seventieth New York
Seventy-Second New York
Seventy-Third New York
Seventy-Fourth New York

Third Brigade: Brigadier General Francis E. Patterson
Fifth New Jersey
Sixty New Jersey
Seventh New Jersey
Eighth New Jersey

Artillery: Major Charles S. Wainwright
First New York Artillery Battery D.
Fourth New York Artillery

Sixth New York Artillery
First U.S. Artillery
Third Division: Brigadier General Phillip Kearny

First Brigade: Brigadier General Charles Jameson
Fifty-Seventh Pennsylvania
Sixty-Third Pennsylvania
105th Pennsylvania
Eighty-Seventh New York

Second Brigade: Brigadier General David B. Birney
Thirty-Eighth New York
Fortieth New York
Third Maine
Fourth Maine

Third Brigade: Brigadier General Hiram G. Berry
Second Michigan
Third Michigan
Fifth Michigan
Thirty-Seventh New York

IV Corps: Brigadier General Erasmus D. Keyes

First Division: Brigadier General Darius N. Couch
Second Brigade: Brigadier General John Peck
Ninety-Third Pennsylvania
Ninety-Eighth Pennsylvania
102nd Pennsylvania
Fifty-Fifth New York
Sixty-Second New York

Second Division: Brigadier General William F. Smith
First Brigade: Brigadier General Winfield Scott Hancock
Fifth Wisconsin Infantry
Forty-Ninth Pennsylvania Infantry
Sixth Maine Infantry
Forty-Third New York

Second Brigade: Brigadier General W. T. H. Brooks
Second Vermont
Third Vermont
Fourth Vermont
Fifth Vermont
Sixth Vermont

Third Brigade: Brigadier General John Davidson
Seventh Maine Infantry
Thirty-Third New York Infantry
Forty-Ninth New York
Seventy-Sixth New York

Third Division: Brigadier General Silas Casey

First Brigade: Brigadier General Henry M. Naglee
Fifty-Second Pennsylvania
104th Pennsylvania
Fifty-Sixth New York
100th New York
Eleventh Maine

Cavalry Division: Brigadier General George Stoneman

Brigade: Brigadier General Philip St. George Cooke
First U.S. Cavalry
Sixth U.S. Cavalry

First Brigade Reserve: Brigadier General William H. Emory
Eighth Illinois Cavalry
Third Pennsylvania Cavalry

Artillery: Lieutenant Colonel William Hays,
Second U.S. Artillery Batteries B, L, M
Third U.S. Artillery Batteries C, K

Appendix D

# THE HOSPITALS OF WILLIAMSBURG

**B**efore the Civil War, hospitals anywhere in America were generally regarded as places for the lower classes who had nowhere else to turn for medical care. They were usually attached to a local almshouse or poorhouse and sometimes to a medical school. Sickness and any emergency medical care was customarily endured at home under the care of relatives, friends or the local physician rather than a hospital.

As the war began, there were five rather small charity hospitals located in the Confederate capital of Richmond, Virginia, and an insignificant Army hospital at Fort Monroe eighty miles to the east on the Virginia Peninsula, with nothing in between. There were no hospitals (in the modern sense of the word) in Williamsburg, but there was the Eastern State Lunatic Asylum, commonly called "the Hospital." The asylum dated to 1773 and was solely for the care of the mentally ill. Although it had considerably grown by 1860, there was no provision for general medical care other than for that of its admitted patients.

With the influx of volunteer soldiers in and around the city in 1861, a Confederate military hospital was established by Letitia Semple in the vacant Williamsburg Female Academy. As that building reached capacity, other hospitals were necessarily established in Williamsburg's churches and at the College of William & Mary.

On May 5, 1862, the town itself became a huge emergency hospital following the battle outside of town. The number of casualties on both sides (almost four thousand killed and wounded) was twice as large as the city's population. As the wounded poured into town, public buildings were quickly filled, and many residents opened their homes for use. Soon, any building that could shelter the wounded from the rain was used as a "hospital." Neither side was medically prepared for the battle; for the first twenty-four hours, there were more "hospitals" than there were military or civilian physicians to staff them. A listing of the known sites in Williamsburg where the wounded were taken includes the following:

Wren Building (College of William & Mary)
Eastern State Lunatic Asylum
Dr. J.M. Galt's House (asylum superintendent's house)
African Baptist Church
Bruton Parish Church
Reverend T. Ambler's house (Episcopal rectory)
City Hotel
Williamsburg Methodist Church
District Courthouse
Williamsburg/James City Courthouse (Courthouse of 1770)
Mr. Harrell's boardinghouse (Chowning's Tavern)
Williamsburg Baptist Church
Hoffheimer store
Mr. W.W. Vest's store (Raleigh Tavern)
Mr. R. Bucktrout's house
Miss E. Morrison's house
Military hospital at Williamsburg Female Academy (Old Capital Site)
Mrs. M. Claibourne's house
Dr. R. Garrett house
Colonel G. Durfey's house (Bassett Hall)
Mrs. E. Ware's house
Mrs. S. Smith's house
Mr. A.G. Southall's house
Mrs. N.B. Tucker's house
Dr. Coleman's house
Mrs. L. Semple's house
Mr. W. Peachy's house
Mr. C. Waller's house
Mr. Hansford's house
Mr. J.T. James's house (James Blair House)
Mrs. King's house

Mr. H. Jones's House
Mrs. C.M. Maupin's house
Mr. Baylor's house
Reverend S.W. Blain's house
Colonel Munford's house (Tazewell Hall)

By its very nature, a battlefield hospital is something that only exists during and immediately after a battle. Most of the locations noted were in use for a week or less. As the Union army entered the city, they took responsibility for the care of all the wounded in town—regardless of the color of their uniforms. Within a short time, most of the wounded had been placed in centralized locations in the larger buildings in town.

Within a week, the main Confederate hospitals were at the Williamsburg Female Academy, the Baptist church on Market Square and Bruton Parish Church. Very quickly, the Federal wounded were taken to U.S. Sanitary Commission steamers on the York River, then to Fort Monroe and points north. Confederate wounded who could be moved were also sent through Fort Monroe as prisoners of war. Severely wounded Confederates were allowed to remain in Williamsburg, and several officers recuperated in various private homes.

There were some wounded still in the city as late as August, when the remaining hospitals were shut down. The Federal garrison at nearby Fort Magruder retained a military hospital at that location for the remainder of the war.

Appendix E

# A NOTE ON MAPS OF
# CIVIL WAR WILLIAMSBURG

## Lost in the Woods

A basic element of any military operation is knowledge of the terrain. This proved to be a huge problem for both Union and Confederate commanders during their armies' maneuvering around Williamsburg in early 1862. The Virginia Peninsula, on which Williamsburg sits, is a thin finger of land bounded on the north by the York River, on the south by the James River and in the east by the Chesapeake Bay. Overall, it is approximately sixty miles long but comparatively narrow, measuring only about seven miles across just east of Williamsburg.

In the twenty-first century, it is well mapped and crisscrossed with highways, secondary roads, directional signs and major bridges. It has even been well detailed by satellite photography. If all else fails, there are plenty of local tourist maps and GPS.

In 1862, it was quite the opposite. There were no up-to-date detailed maps. The area was full of narrow, muddy roads and footpaths on the high ground between innumerable swamps and marshes. In the best of times, they were merely inconvenient; at the worst of times, they were impassable. Attempting to travel any length of ground required a local knowledge of which roads connected to others. Unfortunately, most "local guides" were just that and were usually only familiar with a small area. The quickest and easiest way of travel was by steamboat on either the York or James River, and there were several established boat landings along both rivers.

When Confederate forces occupied the peninsula in 1862, many of the troops came from the Deep South and were just as lost in the area as any

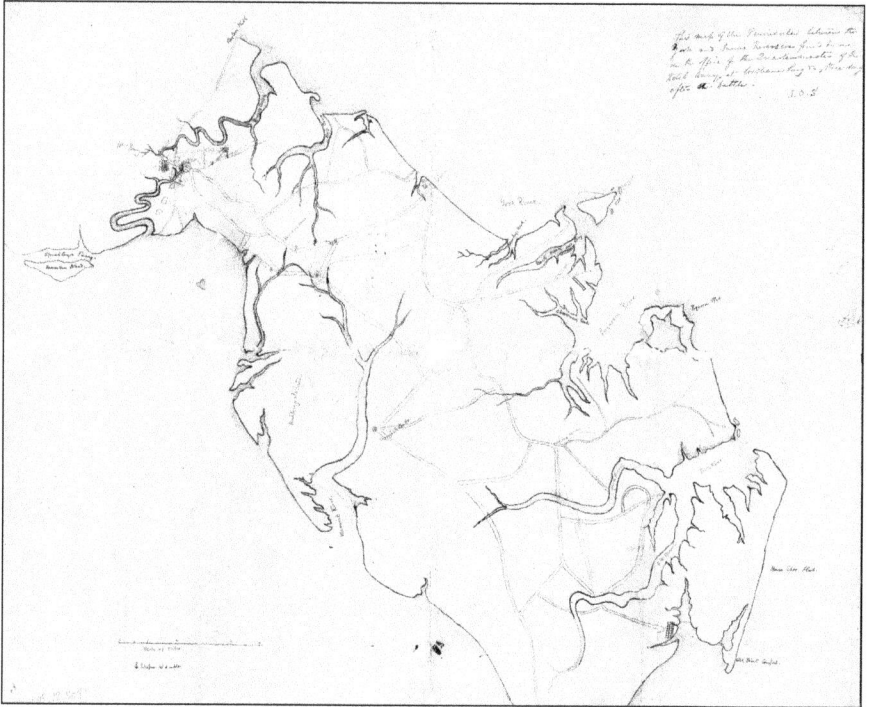

*Above*: This Confederate map of the lower Tidewater Peninsula was found by Federal troops in Williamsburg in May 1862. *Library of Congress.*

*Opposite, top*: A map of southeastern Virginia showing various steamboat routes. Although lacking important detail, it was used by McClellan to plan the Peninsula Campaign. *Library of Congress.*

*Opposite, bottom*: A map of the lower Virginia Peninsula, April 1862. Although it was compiled by Union topographical engineers, it still lacked detail and contained mistakes. *Library of Congress.*

present-day tourists. Confederate general John B. Magruder was quite delighted when Williamsburg resident Sallie Galt furnished a map of the area that had belonged to her grandfather and dated to the 1781 siege of Yorktown. Union general McClellan discovered that the War Department possessed no detailed maps of the area and was forced to buy a steamboat route map in New York City that was less than detailed about land features. Eventually, as troops on both sides floundered about in April and May 1862, military cartographers began to put together acceptable maps. As late as the Battle of Williamsburg, however, the commanders were still relatively in the dark.

Map of the Peninsula of Virginia. Showing route of McClellan's

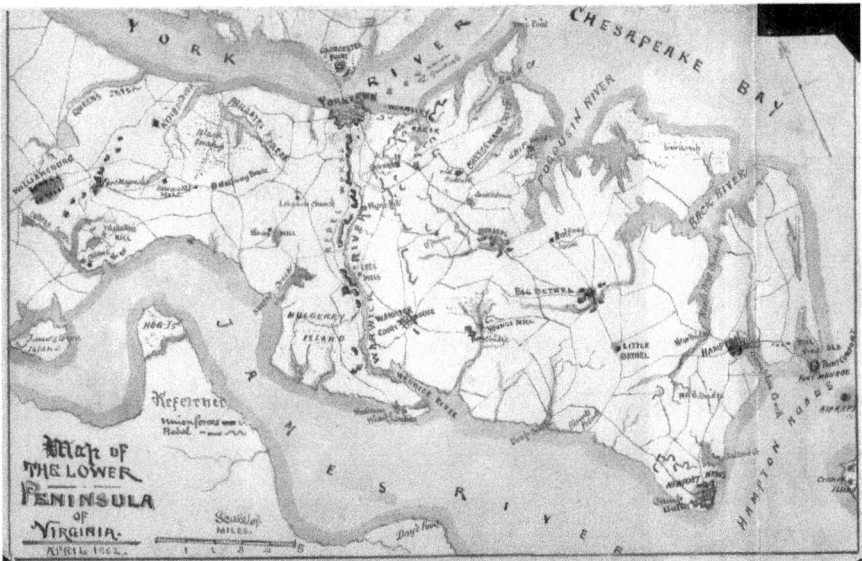

Map of the Lower Peninsula of Virginia. April 1862.

During the battle of May 5, 1862, Confederate general James Longstreet failed to have his troops occupy several earthen forts on his left flank simply because he wasn't aware of their existence. When notified of Union troops occupying these forgotten forts, he ordered General Jubal Early to counter the threat. Early's brigade proceeded to get tangled and lost in the woods, and only half of his men made it to open ground—unfortunately, it was right in front of Union general Winfield Scott Hancock's brigade. The resulting combat on that front was a disaster for the Confederates.

On the Northern side, Hancock's Brigade had made it to that side of the field because of information about a road that was furnished by a contraband slave. The road was on no Union map. Overall, the battle evolved into three disconnected fights for Union commanders all because of lack of knowledge of the terrain.

Appendix F

# THE EMANCIPATION PROCLAMATION

The Emancipation Proclamation presented an unusual legal point in the City of Williamsburg, since the city was spread across two counties with different directives regarding the enforcement of the proclamation. The northern part of the city was in York County, while the southern part of the city and the city courthouse were in James City County. According to a purely technical reading of the proclamation, slaves would have only been freed in the part of Williamsburg that was south of the Duke of Gloucester Street.

The part of the proclamation exempting certain parts of Virginia, including York County, is located in the fifth paragraph. The italics and bolding are the author's. The proclamation reads:

*By the President of the United States of America:*
*A Proclamation.*

*Whereas, on the twenty-second day of September, in the year of our Lord one thousand eight hundred and sixty-two, a proclamation was issued by the President of the United States, containing, among other things, the following, to wit:*
*"That on the first day of January, in the year of our Lord one thousand eight hundred and sixty-three, all persons held as slaves within any State or designated part of a State, the people whereof shall then be in rebellion against the United States, shall be then, thenceforward, and forever free;*

and the Executive Government of the United States, including the military and naval authority thereof, will recognize and maintain the freedom of such persons, and will do no act or acts to repress such persons, or any of them, in any efforts they may make for their actual freedom."

"That the Executive will, on the first day of January aforesaid, by proclamation, designate the States and parts of States, if any, in which the people thereof, respectively, shall then be in rebellion against the United States; and the fact that any State, or the people thereof, shall on that day be, in good faith, represented in the Congress of the United States by members chosen thereto at elections wherein a majority of the qualified voters of such State shall have participated, shall, in the absence of strong countervailing testimony, be deemed conclusive evidence that such State, and the people thereof, are not then in rebellion against the United States."

Now, therefore I, Abraham Lincoln, President of the United States, by virtue of the power in me vested as Commander-in-Chief, of the Army and Navy of the United States in time of actual armed rebellion against the authority and government of the United States, and as a fit and necessary war measure for suppressing said rebellion, do, on this first day of January, in the year of our Lord one thousand eight hundred and sixty-three, and in accordance with my purpose so to do publicly proclaimed for the full period of one hundred days, from the day first above mentioned, order and designate as the States and parts of States wherein the people thereof respectively, are this day in rebellion against the United States, the following, to wit:

Arkansas, Texas, Louisiana, (except the Parishes of St. Bernard, Plaquemines, Jefferson, St. John, St. Charles, St. James Ascension, Assumption, Terrebonne, Lafourche, St. Mary, St. Martin, and Orleans, including the City of New Orleans) Mississippi, Alabama, Florida, Georgia, South Carolina, North Carolina, and Virginia, (except the forty-eight counties designated as West Virginia, and also the counties of Berkley, Accomac, Northampton, Elizabeth City, York, Princess Ann, and Norfolk, including the cities of Norfolk and Portsmouth) and which excepted parts, are for the present, left precisely as if this proclamation were not issued.

And by virtue of the power, and for the purpose aforesaid, I do order and declare that all persons held as slaves within said designated States, and parts of States, are, and henceforward shall be free; and that the Executive government of the United States, including the military and naval authorities thereof, will recognize and maintain the freedom of said persons.

*And I hereby enjoin upon the people so declared to be free to abstain from all violence, unless in necessary self-defense; and I recommend to them that, in all cases when allowed, they labor faithfully for reasonable wages.*

*And I further declare and make known, that such persons of suitable condition, will be received into the armed service of the United States to garrison forts, positions, stations, and other places, and to man vessels of all sorts in said service.*

*And upon this act, sincerely believed to be an act of justice, warranted by the Constitution, upon military necessity, I invoke the considerate judgment of mankind, and the gracious favor of Almighty God.*

*In witness whereof, I have hereunto set my hand and caused the seal of the United States to be affixed.*

*Done at the City of Washington, this first day of January, in the year of our Lord one thousand eight hundred and sixty-three, and of the Independence of the United States of America the eighty-seventh.*

*By the President: ABRAHAM LINCOLN*

*WILLIAM H. SEWARD, Secretary of State*

Appendix G

# THE MEDAL OF HONOR AT WILLIAMSBURG

## *May 5, 1862*

George Washington had created a "Badge of Military Merit" in 1782 in order to recognize military courage; however, none were awarded after the end of the Revolutionary War. In 1847, a Certificate of Military Merit was authorized for the same purpose, but American soldiers really had no medal for valor until the Civil War.

In late 1861, legislation authorized a Navy "medal of honor" that could be awarded to sailors and marines. In February 1862, the army authorized its own version of the medal. The resolution establishing the medal stated that:

> *The President of the United States…is hereby authorized to cause two thousand "medals of honor" to be prepared with suitable emblematic devices, and to direct that the same be presented, in the name of Congress, to such noncommissioned officers and privates as shall most distinguish themselves by their gallantry in action, and other soldier-like qualities during the present insurrection.*

At the Battle of Williamsburg on May 5, 1862, seven Union soldiers were cited for their actions on the field and awarded the medal. Some of the seven were also cited for additional actions during the war. The seven men cited were:

**Robert Milton Boody** (1836–1913), sergeant, Company B, Fortieth New York Infantry
**Citation**: "This soldier, at Williamsburg, Va., then a corporal, at great personal risk, voluntarily saved the lives of and brought from the battlefield 2 wounded comrades. A year later, at Chancellorsville, voluntarily, and at great personal risk, brought from the field of battle and saved the life of Captain George B. Carse, Company C, 40th New York Volunteer Infantry."

**Martin Conboy** (1833–1909), sergeant, Company B, Thirty-Seventh New York Infantry
**Citation**: "Took command of the company in action, the captain having been wounded, the other commissioned officers being absent, and handled it with skill and bravery."

**John Nicholas Coyne** (1839–1907), sergeant, Company B, Seventieth New York Infantry
**Citation**: "Capture of a flag after a severe hand-to-hand contest; was mentioned in orders for his gallantry."

**Michael A. Dillon** (1839–1904), private, Company G, Second New Hampshire Infantry
**Citation**: "Bravery in repulsing the enemy's charge on a battery, at Williamsburg, Va. At Oak Grove, Va., crawled outside the lines and brought in important information."

**Thomas Timothy Fallon** (1837–1916), private, Company K, Thirty-Seventh New York Infantry
**Citation**: "At Williamsburg, Va., assisted in driving rebel skirmishers to their main line. Participated in action, at Fair Oaks, Va., though excused from duty because of disability. In a charge with his company at Big Shanty, Ga., was the first man on the enemy's works."

**John H. Haight** (1841–1917), sergeant, Company G, Seventy-Second New York Infantry
**Citation**: "At Williamsburg, Va., voluntarily carried a severely wounded comrade off the field in the face of a large force of the enemy; in doing so was himself severely wounded and taken prisoner. Went into the fight at Bristol Station, Va., although severely disabled. At Manassas, volunteered to search the woods for the wounded."

**George W. Mindil** (1841–1907), captain, Company I, Sixty-First Pennsylvania Infantry

**Citation**: "As aide-de-camp led the charge with a part of a regiment, pierced the enemy's center, silenced some of his artillery, and, getting in his rear, caused him to abandon his position."

# BIBLIOGRAPHY

## Books and Articles

Beatie, Russel H. *Army of the Potomac, Vol III: McClellan's First Campaign March–May 1862*. New York: Savas Beatie, 2007.

Bellard, Alfred. *Gone For a Soldier: The Civil War Memoirs of Private Alfred Bellard*. Edited by David Herbert Donald. Boston: Little, Brown and Company, 1975.

Bergeron, Arthur W. Jr. *Guide to Louisiana Confederate Military Units 1861–1865*. Baton Rouge: Louisiana State University, 1989.

Blake, Henry N. *Three Years in the Army of the Potomac*. Boston: Lee and Shepard, 1865.

Brasher, Glenn D. *The Peninsula Campaign & the Necessity of Emancipation: African Americans and the Fight for Freedom*. Chapel Hill: University of North Carolina Press, 2012.

Bright, Robert Southall. *Memories of Williamsburg and Stories of My Father*. Richmond, VA: Garrett & Massie, 1941.

*Bruton Parish Churchyard and Church: A Guide to the Tombstones, Monuments, and Mural Tablets*. Williamsburg, VA: Bruton Parish Church, 1976.

Burns, James R. *The Battle of Williamsburgh, With Reminiscences of the Campaign, Hospital Experiences, Debates, Etc*. New York: Self-published, 1865.

Burton, Brian K. *The Peninsula & Seven Days: A Battlefield Guide*. Lincoln: University of Nebraska Press, 2007.

Calcutt, Rebecca Barbour. *Richmond's Wartime Hospitals*. Gretna, LA: Pelican Publishing, 2005.

Casdorph, Paul D. *Prince John Magruder: His Life and Campaigns*. New York: John Wiley & Sons, Inc., 1996.

Comte de Paris. *History of the Civil War in America*, Vol. II. Philadelphia: Porter and Coates, 1876.

*Confederate Veteran*. Nashville, TN: Vol. 1–40, 1893–1932.

Crute, Joseph, Jr. *Units of the Confederate Army*. Midlothian, VA: Derwent Books, 1987.

Cunningham, Horace H. *Doctors in Gray: The Confederate Medical Service*. Baton Rouge: Louisiana State University Press, 1958.

————. *Field Medical Services at the Battles of Manassas*. Athens: University of Georgia Press, 1968.

Custer, George A. *Custer in the Civil War: His Unfinished Memoirs*. Edited by John M. Carroll. San Rafael, CA: Presidio Press, 1977.

Dain, Norman. *Disordered Minds: The First Century of Eastern State Hospital in Williamsburg, Virginia, 1766–1866*. Williamsburg, VA: Colonial Williamsburg Foundation, 1971.

Davis, Jefferson. *The Rise and Fall of the Confederate Government*, 2 vols. New York: D. Appleton & Co., 1881.

Dougherty, Kevin, and J. Michael Moore. *The Peninsula Campaign of 1862: A Military Analysis*. Jackson: University Press of Mississippi, 2005.

Dubbs, Carol Kettenburg. *Defend This Old Town: Williamsburg during the Civil War*. Baton Rouge: Louisiana State University Press, 2002.

Evans, Charles M. *War of the Aeronauts: A History of Ballooning in the Civil War*. Mechanicsburg, PA: Stackpole, 2002.

Eyland, Seth (pseudonym of David E. Cronin). *The Evolution of a Life: Described in the Memoirs of Major Seth Eyland*. New York: S.W. Green's Son, 1884.

Faust, Patricia L., ed. *Historical Times Illustrated Encyclopedia of the Civil War*. New York: Harper and Row, 1986.

Fleming, Francis P. *Memoir of Capt. C. Seton Fleming, of the Second Florida Infantry, C.S.A.* Jacksonville, FL: Times-Union Publishing House, 1884.

Freeman, Douglas Southall. *Lee's Lieutenants: A Study in Command*. 3 vols. New York: Charles Scribner's Sons, 1942.

Goodwin, Rutherford. *Williamsburg in Virginia*. 3rd ed. Richmond, VA: Dietz Press, 1980.

Hagemann, James. *The Heritage of Virginia: The Story of Place Names In The Old Dominion*. 2nd ed. Norfolk, VA: Donning Company, 1988.

Hall, Richard. *Patriots in Disguise: Women Warriors of the Civil War*. New York: Marlowe and Company, 1994.

Hastings, Earl C., Jr., and David Hastings. *A Pitiless Rain: The Battle of Williamsburg, 1862*. Shippensburg, PA: White Mane Publishing, 1997.

Hess, Earl J. *Field Armies and Fortifications in the Civil War: The Eastern Campaigns, 1861–1864*. Chapel Hill: University of North Carolina, 2005.

Heuvel, Sean, and Lisa L. Heuvel. *The College of William & Mary in the Civil War*. Jefferson, NC: McFarland & Company Inc., 2013.

Hudson, Carson O., Jr. *Civil War Williamsburg*. Williamsburg, VA: Colonial Williamsburg Foundation, 1997.

———. "Red Legged Devils Visit Virginia's Peninsula." *Colonial Williamsburg Journal* 23, no. 3 (Summer 2005): 72–77.

———. "'We Bow Our Heads to Yankee Despotism': Occupied Williamsburg in the War Between the States." *Colonial Williamsburg Journal* 22, no. 2 (Summer 2000): 56–62.

Hume, Ivor Noel. *Something From the Cellar: More of This & That*. Williamsburg, VA: Colonial Williamsburg Foundation, 2005.

Jackson, William J. *New Jerseyans in the Civil War: For Union and Liberty*. New Brunswick, NJ: Rutgers University Press, 2006.

Jensen, Les. *32nd Virginia Infantry*. Lynchburg, VA: H.E. Howard, Inc., 1990.

Jones, Terry L. *Lee's Tigers: The Louisiana Infantry in the Army of Northern Virginia*. Baton Rouge: Louisiana State Press, 1987.

Jordan, David M. *Winfield Scott Hancock: A Soldier's Life*. Indianapolis: Indiana University Press, 1988.

Jordan, Ervin L., Jr. *Black Confederates and Afro-Yankees in Civil War Virginia*. Charlottesville: University Press of Virginia, 1995.

Kinsley, D.A. *Favor the Bold*. New York: Holt, Rinehart and Winston, 1967.

Kreutzer, William. *Notes and Observations Made During Four Years of Service with the Ninety-Eighth N.Y. Volunteers in the War of 1861*. Philadelphia: Grant, Faires & Rodgers, 1878.

Krick, Robert K. *Civil War Weather in Virginia*. Tuscaloosa: University of Alabama Press, 2007.

———. *Lee's Colonels: A Biographical Register of Field Officers of the Army of Northern Virginia*. 4th ed. Dayton, OH: Morningside House, Inc., 1992.

Lindgren, James M. *Preserving the Old Dominion: Historic Preservation and Virginia Traditionalism*. Charlottesville: University Press of Virginia, 1993.

Lively, E.H. "Williamsburg Junior Guards." *Southern Historical Society Papers*, vol. 18 (1890): 275–77.

Lowe, Richard. *Republicans and Reconstruction in Virginia, 1856–70.* Charlottesville: University Press of Virginia, 1991.

Marks, James J. *The Peninsular Campaign in Virginia or Incidents and Scenes on the Battlefields and in Richmond.* Philadelphia: J.B. Lippincott & Co., 1864.

Maury, Richard L. *The Battle of Williamsburg and the Charge of the Twenty-Fourth Virginia of Early's Brigade.* Richmond, VA: Johns and Goolsby, 1880.

McClellan, George B. *McClellan's Own Story: The War for the Union.* New York: C.L. Webster and Co., 1887.

McKinney, E.P. *Life in Tent and Field, 1861–1865.* Boston: Gorham Press, 1922.

McMahon, Tom. "The Flag of the 5th North Carolina, the First Southern Banner Captured in the East, Has Been Rediscovered." *America's Civil War* (May 2002): 66.

Meredith, Roy. *Mr. Lincoln's Cameraman: Mathew B. Brady.* 2nd revised ed. New York: Dover Publications, 1974.

Moore, J. Staunton. "An Address Delivered by J. Staunton Moore at the 50th Re-union of the Fifteenth Virginia Regiment at Williamsburg, Virginia on May 24, 1911." n.d.

Newton, Steven H. *Joseph E. Johnston and the Defense of Richmond.* Lawrence: University Press of Kansas, 1998.

Nine, William G., and Ronald G. Wilson. *The Appomattox Paroles April 9–15, 1865.* 3rd ed. Lynchburg, VA: H.E. Howard, Inc., 1989.

Nolan, Dick. *Benjamin Franklin Butler: The Damnedest Yankee.* Novato, CA: Presidio Press, 1991.

Olmert, Michael. *Official Guide to Colonial Williamsburg.* Williamsburg, VA: Colonial Williamsburg Foundation, 1985.

Perdue, Charles L., Jr., Thomas E. Barden and Robert K. Phillips, eds. *Weevils in the Wheat: Interviews with Virginia Ex-Slaves.* Charlottesville: University of Virginia Press, 1976.

Pratt, Fletcher. *Civil War in Pictures.* Garden City, NY: Garden City Books, 1955.

Priest, John Michael, ed. *One Surgeon's Private War: Doctor William W. Potter of the 57th New York.* Shippensburg, PA: White Mane Publishing Co., Inc., 1996.

Quarstein, John V., and J. Michael Moore. *Yorktown's Civil War Siege: Drums Along the Warwick.* Charleston, SC: The History Press, 2012.

*Registers of Deaths in the Regular Army, 1860–1889.* 18 vols. Records of the Adjutant General's Office. Record Group 94. National Archives, Washington, D.C.

Robertson, William Glenn. *Back Door to Richmond: The Bermuda Hundred Campaign April–June 1864.* Baton Rouge: Louisiana State University, 1987.

Robinson, Dale G. *The Academies of Virginia, 1776–1861*. Richmond, VA: Dietz Press, 1977.

Rouse, Parke, Jr. *Cows on the Campus: Williamsburg in Bygone Days*. Richmond, VA: Dietz Press, 1973.

———. *Remembering Williamsburg: A Sentimental Journey through Three Centuries*. Richmond, VA: Dietz Press, 1989.

Salmon, Emily J., and Edward D.C. Campbell Jr., eds. *Hornbook of Virginia History*. 4th ed. Richmond: Library of Virginia, 1994.

Seager, Robert, II. *And Tyler Too: A Biography of John and Julia Gardiner Tyler*. New York: McGraw-Hill, 1963.

Sears, Stephen W. *To the Gates of Richmond: The Peninsula Campaign*. New York: Ticknor and Fields, 1992.

Simkins, Francis B., and James W. Patton. *The Women of the Confederacy*. Richmond, VA: Garrett and Massie Inc., 1936.

Styple, William B., ed. *Letters from the Peninsula: The Civil War Letters of General Philip Kearny*. Kearny, NJ: Belle Grove Publishing, 1988.

Symonds, Craig L. *Joseph E. Johnston: A Civil War Biography*. New York: W.W. Norton & Co., 1992.

Thomas, Emory M. *Bold Dragoon: The Life of J.E.B. Stuart*. New York: Harper & Row, 1986.

Thomason, John W., Jr. *JEB Stuart*. New York: Mallard Press, 1992.

Tucker, Beverly D. *Nathaniel Beverly Tucker: Prophet of the Confederacy 1784–1851*. Tokyo: Nan'Un-Do, 1979.

Tucker, Beverly Randolph. *Tales of the Tuckers: Descendants of the Male Line of St. George Tucker of Bermuda and Virginia*. Richmond, VA: Dietz Printing Co., 1942.

U.S. Bureau of the Census. City of Williamsburg and James City County. 1860. Microfilm.

U.S. War Department. *Revised United States Army Regulations of 1861*. Washington: Government Printing Office, 1863.

———. *The War of the Rebellion: A Compilation of the Official Records of the Union and Confederate Armies*. 70 vols. and atlas. Washington, D.C.: Government Printing Office, 1880–1901.

Wallace, Lee A., Jr. *A Guide to Virginia Military Organizations, 1861–1865*. 2nd revised ed. Lynchburg, VA: H.E. Howard, Inc., 1986.

———. *Surry Light Artillery and Martin's, Wright's, Coffin's Batteries of Virginia Artillery*. Lynchburg, VA: H.E. Howard, Inc., 1995.

Warner, Ezra J. *Generals in Blue: Lives of the Union Commanders*. Baton Rouge: Louisiana State University Press, 1964.

———. *Generals in Gray: Lives of the Confederate Commanders*. Baton Rouge: Louisiana State University Press, 1959.

Webb, Alexander S. *The Peninsula: McClellan's Campaign of 1862*. Vol. III of *Campaigns of the Civil War*. New York: Charles Scribner's Sons, 1882.

Welsh, Jack D. *Medical Histories of Confederate Generals*. Kent, OH: Kent State University Press, 1995.

———. *Medical Histories of Union Generals*. Kent, OH: Kent State University Press, 1996.

Werstein, Irving. *Kearny the Magnificent: The Story of General Philip Kearny 1815–1862*. New York: John Day Co., 1962.

Wert, Jeffrey D. *Custer: The Controversial Life of George Armstrong Custer*. New York: Simon & Schuster, 1996.

West, George Benjamin. *When the Yankees Came: Civil War and Reconstruction on the Virginia Peninsula*. Edited by Parke Rouse Jr. Richmond, VA: Dietz Press, 1977.

Wheelan, Joseph. *Libbie Prison Breakout: The Daring Escape from the Notorious Civil War Prison*. New York: Public Affairs, 2010.

Wheeler, Richard. *Sword over Richmond: An Eyewitness History of McClellan's Peninsula Campaign*. New York: Harper and Row, 1986.

Wiatt, Alex L. *26th Virginia Infantry*. Lynchburg, VA: H.E. Howard, Inc., 1984.

Willet, Robert L. *One Day of the Civil War: America in Conflict April 10, 1863*. New York: Plume, Penguin Group, 1998.

Williamsburg Garden Club. *Williamsburg Scrap Book*. Richmond, VA: Dietz Printing Co., 1937.

Wilson, Robert. *Mathew Brady: Portraits of a Nation*. New York: Bloomsbury, 2013.

Work Projects Administration Writers' Program. *The Negro in Virginia*. Winston-Salem: John F. Blair, publisher, 1994.

Worman, Charles G. *Civil War Animal Heroes: Mascots, Pets and War Horses*. Lynchburg, VA: Schroeder Publications, 2011.

Yetter, George H. *Williamsburg Before and After: The Rebirth of Virginia's Colonial Capital*. Williamsburg: Colonial Williamsburg Foundation, 1988.

## Newspapers

*The Cavalier*, 1862
*Richmond Daily Enquirer*, 1861–65
*Richmond Dispatch*, 1861–65
*Richmond Enquirer*, 1861–65

*Virginia Gazette*, 1853–57
*Williamsburg Weekly Gazette and Eastern Virginia Advertiser*, 1859–60

## Unpublished Manuscripts and Sources

Baker, Eliza. Interview transcript. Williamsburg, May 4, 1933. Colonial Williamsburg Research Library, Williamsburg, VA.

Bright, Robert Anderson, 1839–1904. "Autobiographical Essay of Robert Anderson Bright," John D. Rockefeller Jr. Library, Colonial Williamsburg Foundation, accessed June 9, 2015, https://rocklib.omeka.net/items/show/7.

Cary, Harriette. Diary. Special Collections, Earl Greg Swem Library, College of William & Mary, Williamsburg, VA.

Charles, John S. "Recollections of Williamsburg, Virginia, As It Appeared at the Beginning of the Civil War." Manuscript. Colonial Williamsburg Foundation Research Library, Williamsburg, VA.

Coleman, Cynthia B.T. "My Peninsula Campaign." Manuscript. Colonial Williamsburg Foundation Research Library, Williamsburg, VA.

Coleman-Washington Papers. Microfilm. Colonial Williamsburg Foundation Research Library. Original in Earl Greg Swem Library, College of William & Mary, Williamsburg, VA.

Cronin, David E. "The Vest Mansion: Its Historical and Romantic Associations as Confederate and Union Headquarters (1862–1865) in the American Civil War." Manuscript. Colonial Williamsburg Foundation Research Library, Williamsburg, VA.

Dorsey-Copeland Papers. Special Collections, Earl Greg Swem Library, College of William & Mary, Williamsburg, VA.

Eastern State Hospital Records, Special Collections Research Center, Swem Library, College of William & Mary, Williamsburg, VA.

Galt Family Papers. Special Collections, Earl Greg Swem Library, College of William & Mary, Williamsburg, VA.

Lee, Victoria King. "Williamsburg in 1861." Manuscript. Colonial Williamsburg Foundation Research Library, Williamsburg, VA.

Vandegrift, Martha. Interview transcript. Gloucester Co., April 23, 1932. Colonial Williamsburg Research Library, Williamsburg, VA.

William & Mary Papers. Special Collections, Earl Greg Swem Library, College of William & Mary, Williamsburg, VA.

## *Illustrations*

Library and Archives Canada
Library of Congress Geography and Map Division, Washington, D.C.
Library of Congress Prints and Photographs Division, Washington, D.C.
Missouri Historical Society
National Archives and Records Administration, Washington, D.C.
Rockefeller Library, Colonial Williamsburg Foundation, Williamsburg, Virginia
Wikimedia Commons Public Domain

# INDEX

## A

Abraham, Thomas, Private (USA)
150
Adams, John Quincy 49
African Baptist Church 208
Ambler, Thomas M., Reverend 54,
126, 153
Anderson, Helen Maxwell 123,
124, 125
Anthony Hay Shop 74
Appomattox, Virginia 77, 111, 138,
153, 156, 159, 199
Aub, Jacob 101, 103
August, Thomas, Colonel (CSA) 33

## B

Badham, John C., Lieutenant
Colonel (CSA) 106
Baker, Eliza 119

Baldwin, Charles, Private (USA)
99, 100
battles
Big Bethel 33, 97
Big Shanty 220
Bristol Station 220
Chancellorsville 111, 220
Chantilly 60
Chickamauga 64
Dinwiddie Courthouse 79
Fair Oaks 220
Five Forks 78
Fort Sumter 16
Frayser's Farm 77
Gettysburg 64, 77, 79
Little Bighorn 112, 113, 114
Malvern Hill 33, 59
Manassas 45, 52, 61, 98, 107,
220
New Orleans 92
Oak Grove 220
Second Manassas 59, 77, 100

Seven Pines 108

Williamsburg 13, 24, 48, 54, 55, 64, 70, 72, 75, 77, 89, 99, 112, 117, 151, 212, 219, 220

Winchester 79, 111

Baylor House 209

Bellard, Alfred, Private (USA) 14

Belle Isle 147, 148

Blain House 209

Blake, Henry, Captain (USA) 15, 65

Boody, Robert Milton, Sergeant (USA) 220

Bowden, Henry 92, 94

Bowden, Lemuel Jackson 92, 93, 94

Bowden, Mary 93, 94, 95

Bowden, Mildred 92, 95

Bowden, Thomas 94, 95

Boyle, William, Private (USA) 145, 146, 147, 149, 150

Brady, Matthew 49, 50, 51

Bright, Robert Anderson, Captain (CSA) 159

Brown, John 41, 85, 197

Bruton Parish Church 51, 54, 70, 92, 133, 153, 209

Buchanan, James 41

Bucktrout House 208

Busteed, Richard, General (USA) 127, 128, 130, 131

Butler, Benjamin, General (USA) 90, 91, 97, 116, 147, 149, 150

**C**

Campbell, Billy, Private (CSA) 26, 28

Campbell, David, Colonel (USA) 120, 124, 152

Carse, George B., Captain (USA) 220

Cary, Harriette 14, 81, 94, 108

Charles, John S. 19, 83

City Hotel 26, 208

Claiborne, Mary 66, 67

Claibourne House 208

Clay, Henry 49

Coleman, Charles, Dr. (CSA) 47

Coleman, Cynthia Beverly Tucker 14, 17, 54, 66, 68, 69, 70, 84, 121, 129, 138, 157

Coleman House 208

College of William & Mary 13, 17, 21, 24, 32, 34, 51, 59, 76, 85, 87, 92, 120, 121, 136, 143, 153, 154, 159, 197, 198, 207

Colonial Williamsburg 9, 24, 74, 100, 226

Conboy, Martin, Sergeant (USA) 220

Coupland, John 133

Coyne, John Nicholas, Sergeant (USA) 220

Cronin, David, Major (USA) 139, 140, 141, 143, 144

Cullen, J.S.D., Dr. (CSA) 70

Custer, George Armstrong, Lieutenant (USA) 106, 107, 108, 110, 111, 112, 113, 114

**D**

Davis, Jefferson 29, 30, 37, 40, 54, 145, 149

Davis, William J., Private (CSA) 67

DeGourney, Paul, Lieutenant Colonel (CSA) 43

Dillon, Michael A., Private (USA) 220

Disosway, William W., Lieutenant (USA) 145, 146

District Courthouse 208

Dix, Dorothea 90, 91

Dix, John A., General (USA) 105, 124, 125, 127, 130

Duke of Gloucester Street 14, 126

Durfey, Goodrich 108, 133

Durfey House 110, 208

Durfey, Margaret 108, 110, 111

Duryee, Abram, Colonel (USA) 96, 97, 98


E

Early, Jubal A., General (CSA) 54, 76, 79, 105, 107, 214

Eastern State Lunatic Asylum 19, 22, 24, 45, 51, 87, 89, 90, 94, 115, 125, 151, 152, 153, 207, 208

Edmonds, Sarah Emma 61, 62

Episcopal rectory 208

Ewell, Benjamin, Colonel (CSA) 17, 19, 30, 59, 198

Ewell, Rebecca 59

Ewell, Richard, General (CSA) 17, 59


F

Fallon, Thomas Timothy, Private (USA) 220

Flanagan, H.M., Corporal (USA) 125

Fleming, Charles S., Lieutenant (CSA) 66, 67

Fleming, Francis, Private (CSA) 66, 67

Forney, William Henry, Captain (CSA) 76, 77

Fort Magruder 42, 43, 51, 126, 133, 144, 146, 147, 153, 157, 209

Fort Monroe 24, 37, 50, 61, 71, 76, 90, 91, 96, 98, 105, 110, 111, 116, 127, 137, 147, 207, 209

Freedmen's Bureau 62, 157


G

Galt, Alexander D. 87, 89

Galt, Alexander, Jr. 87, 88

Galt, Elizabeth Judith 87, 88

Galt, John Minson 87

Galt, John Minson, II 87, 89, 151

Galt, Maria Dorothea 87, 88

Galt, Sarah (Sallie) Maria 19, 87, 88, 89, 90, 91, 105, 123, 133, 152, 212

Gannon, Austin, Private (USA) 154, 155, 156

Garland, Samuel, Jr., Colonel (CSA) 77

Garrett House 208

Garrett, Robert, Dr. 30, 94

Gibson, James 50

Grand Army of the Republic 63

Grant, Ulysses S., General (USA) 73, 154

# H

Haight, John H., Sergeant (USA) 220
Hampton Road 41, 56
Hampton, Virginia 35, 50, 66, 77, 78, 88, 97, 105, 116
Hancock, Winfield Scott, General (USA) 59, 64, 76, 105, 107, 214
Hansford House 208
Harrell's Boarding House 208
Harris, Nathaniel H., Captain (CSA) 77
Heintzelman, Samuel, General (USA) 57
Hennessey, T., Captain (USA) 125
Henry, Patrick 23
Hill, Ambrose Powell, General (CSA) 104
Hill, Daniel H., General (CSA) 104
Hitchcock, Alfred, Dr. (USA) 71
Hoffheimer Store 208
Hooker, Joseph, General (USA) 56, 57, 58, 113

# J

Jackson, Andrew 49
Jackson, Thomas J. ("Stonewall") 73
James House 208
Jefferson, Thomas 142, 144
Johnston, Joseph E., General (CSA) 37, 40, 41, 43, 44, 46, 48, 64, 81, 82
Jones House 209

# K

Kearny, Philip, Jr., General (USA) 55, 56, 58, 59, 60, 62, 113
Kearny, Stephen W. 55
Kilpatrick, Judson, General (USA) 150
King House 208
Kingsmill Wharf 43
King, Victoria 45, 81, 84
Kreutzer, William, Colonel (USA) 64, 65

# L

Lea, John Willis, Captain (CSA) 106, 108, 110, 111
Lee, Arthur 144
Lee, Charles 144
Lee, Richard Henry 143, 144
Lee, Robert E., General (CSA) 40, 41, 73, 78, 94, 104, 111, 138, 147, 155, 157
Letcher, John 16, 19
Libby Prison 147, 148, 150
Lincoln, Abraham 16, 59, 78, 90, 92, 147, 149
Lively, Edward 85
Lively, Mary 85, 86
Lively, Robert 85
Longstreet, James, General (CSA) 44, 48, 104, 132, 214

# M

Madison, James 144

Magruder, John B., General (CSA) 26, 28, 82, 88, 212

Marks, James J., Chaplain (USA) 72

Maupin House 209

McClellan, George B., General (USA) 13, 37, 40, 46, 48, 50, 59, 61, 62, 81, 82, 83, 84, 93, 94, 98, 99, 104, 105, 108, 124, 149, 212

McLaws, Lafayette, General (CSA) 23, 26, 47

Medal of Honor. *See* Appendix G

Melton, Susie 118

Military District Number 1 157

military units

Confederate

2nd Florida Infantry 52, 53, 54, 66

2nd Mississippi Battalion 52

3rd Virginia Cavalry 31

4th Virginia Cavalry 77

5th North Carolina Infantry 105, 106, 108, 111

8th Virginia Infantry 47

10th Alabama Infantry 76

11th Virginia Infantry 77

14th Louisiana Infantry 79

15th Virginia Infantry 32, 33, 34

18th Virginia Infantry 67

19th Mississippi Infantry 77

24th Virginia Infantry 78, 105

26th Virginia Infantry 132

32nd Virginia Infantry 24, 159, 198

43rd Battalion Virginia Cavalry 155

59th Virginia Infantry 126

68th Regiment Virginia Militia 197

Coppens' Battalion 24, 32

DeGourney's Independent Battalion of Heavy Artillery 43

James City Artillery 19

James City Cavalry 19

Peninsula Light Artillery 159

Prospect Rifle Grays 67

Williamsburg Junior Guard 85, 197, 198, 199. *See* Appendix B

Federal

1st New Jersey Brigade 56

1st New York Cavalry 145

1st New York Mounted Rifles 139, 143, 145, 148, 149, 150

1st U.S. Cavalry 41, 112, 113

2nd Michigan Infantry 61, 62

2nd New Hampshire Infantry 220

2nd U.S. Dragoons 55

3rd New York Cavalry 148

5th New Jersey Infantry 14

5th New York Infantry (Duryee's Zouaves) 96, 98, 99

5th Pennsylvania Cavalry 85, 101, 102, 103, 120, 151

5th U.S. Cavalry 107

7th U.S. Cavalry 112, 113, 114

11th Massachusetts Infantry 15

11th Pennsylvania Cavalry 148

13th New York Heavy Artillery 114

16th New York Artillery 154, 156

25th Massachusetts Infantry
142
37th New York Infantry 113,
220
40th New York Infantry 220
49th New York Infantry 70
61st Pennsylvania Infantry 221
70th New York Infantry 220
72nd New York Infantry 220
98th New York Infantry 64, 93
139th New York Volunteers
150
Flint Union Greys 61
U.S. Mounted Rifles 41
U.S. Naval Brigade 114
U.S. Telegraphic Corps 40
other
Chasseurs d'Afrique 55
Mills, Luther R., Lieutenant (CSA)
132
Milton, John 54
Mindil, George W., Captain (USA)
221
Moore, J. Staunton 34
Morrison, Cate 33
Morrison, Catherine Heth 32, 33,
34
Morrison, Emily 67, 68, 129, 133
Morrison House 208
Morrison, Robert J., Captain (CSA)
32, 33
Morrison, Thomas 33
Morse, William, Captain (USA) 61,
62
Mosby, John S., Colonel (CSA) 155
Munford, Mrs. M.N. 117
Murray, Thomas, Private (USA)
113, 114

N

Naglee, Henry M., General (USA)
117
newspapers
*Eastern Virginia Advertiser and Weekly
Gazette* 85
*New York Times* 98
*Richmond Dispatch* 85
*Richmond Enquirer* 20
*Cavalier, The* 85, 86, 102
*Virginia Gazette* 85, 143

O

Old By Jucks 83

P

Page, John 142, 143, 144
Page, John, Mrs. 144
Payne, Mary 78
Payne, William H.F., Major (CSA)
43, 77, 78, 79
Peachy House 208
Peachy, William 77
Pendleton, E.S., Dr. (CSA) 77
Phelps, Ned, Private (CSA) 26
Pickett, George, General (CSA)
159
Pierce, Franklin 56
Poe, Edgar Allan 49
Porter, Charles 94
Potter, William W., Dr. (USA) 70
Putnam, Sam, Private (USA) 142,
143, 144

## R

Randolph, George W. 40
Randolph, Peyton 77, 144
Reno, Marcus A., Captain (USA)
    112, 113, 114
Richards, Thomas W.T., Captain
    (CSA) 155
Rollerson, Roctilda 117

## S

Saunders House 119
Saunders, Robert 143
Scott, Winfield, General (USA) 55,
    56
Seelye, Linus H. 62
Semple House 208
Semple, James 22
Semple, Letitia Tyler 22, 23, 24,
    69, 70, 207
Sherman, William T., General
    (USA) 154
Shultz, E., Lieutenant (USA) 125
Smith House 208
Smith, Meriwether 144
Smith, William T., General (USA)
    107
Southall House 208
Southall, Mary 120
Southall, Travis, Sergeant (CSA)
    29, 30, 31
Southall, Virginia 29, 30, 31
Stoneman, George, General (USA)
    40, 81, 112
Stuart, James Ewell Brown (J.E.B.),
    General (CSA) 40, 41, 43,
    48, 112

Sykes, George, General (USA) 98

## T

Tazewell Hall 26, 209
Terry, Alfred, General (USA) 114
Terry, William R., Colonel (CSA)
    78, 79
Thompson, Franklin 61, 62. *See*
    Edmonds, Sarah Emma
Tiebout, George, Private (USA) 97
Tucker, Cynthia Beverly 47. *See*
    Coleman, Cynthia Beverly
    Tucker
Tucker, Henrietta Elizabeth Beverly
    (Zettie) 138
Tucker House 47, 208
Tucker, Lucy 138
Tucker, Nathaniel Beverly 17
Tucker, St. George 17
Tyler, John 16

## U

U.S. Christian Commission 62
U.S. Sanitary Commission 62, 209

## V

Vest House 82, 145
Vest Store 208

# W

Wager, Peter, Dr. (USA) 151, 152, 153
Walker, Pope 22, 31
Wallace, Gustavus A., Captain (CSA) 126
Waller House 208
Ward, George Taliaferro, Colonel (CSA) 52, 53, 54
Ware House 208
Washington, George 17, 37, 87, 89, 90, 108, 144, 219
Washington, James B., Lieutenant (CSA) 108
Washington, Martha 144
Webster, Daniel 49
West, Robert M., Colonel (USA) 147, 148
Wheelan, James, Major (USA) 148, 149, 228
Whiting, Christopher 121
Wickham, Williams Carter, Lieutenant Colonel (CSA) 41, 42, 43, 79, 80
Williamsburg Baptist Church 66, 68, 208, 209
Williamsburg Battlefield Association 153
Williamsburg Courthouse 21, 53, 208
Williamsburg Female Academy 13, 22, 23, 24, 67, 69, 133, 207, 208, 209
Williamsburg Methodist Church 208
Wise, Henry A., General (CSA) 132, 135, 152

Wistar, Isaac J., General (USA) 145, 147, 148, 149, 150
Wood, John 50
Woodpecker Lane 133

# Y

Yorktown Road 40, 41, 42, 43
Yorktown, Virginia 21, 31, 35, 36, 37, 40, 50, 54, 62, 64, 86, 88, 98, 99, 112, 137, 147, 157
York, Zebulon, Lieutenant Colonel (CSA) 79

# ABOUT THE AUTHOR

Carson Hudson has been passionate about history since he was a young boy growing up in Virginia surrounded by Civil War battlefields. He is a practicing military and social historian, author, Emmy Award–winning screenwriter and circus fire-eater. He regularly lectures on a wide variety of subjects, but his particular interests are the Civil War and colonial witchcraft. He performs regularly as part of the old-time music duo Hudson & Clark and with the Cigar Box String Band. In his spare time, he likes to sleep.

*Visit us at*
www.historypress.com
......................................................

www.ingramcontent.com/pod-product-compliance
Lightning Source LLC
Chambersburg PA
CBHW070359100426
42812CB00005B/1569